CONTENTS

INTRODUCTION

Caledonian MacBrayne Limited was formed on 1 January 1973 by the merger of the two state-owned passenger shipping and ferry operators on the west coast of Scotland: the Caledonian Steam Packet Co. Ltd, which had been formed in 1889 as a subsidiary of the Caledonian Railway and operated services on the Firth of Clyde, and also the Kyle of Lochalsh to Kyleakin ferry service and David MacBrayne Ltd, whose origins went as far back as 1851, and operated in the West Highlands and Islands. Eighteen vessels came into the fleet from the CSP and seventeen from MacBraynes.

The conversion of car ferry routes to roll-on/roll-off operation, which had started in 1970 with the Ardrossan–Brodick service, continued apace with the provision of linkspans and slipways throughout the major route network being completed by 2004. A network of short-distance ferry routes, mainly serving the smaller islands, was developed using slipways rather than linkspans. The excursion sailings on the Clyde and from Oban were reduced and eventually ceased as the older steam-powered vessels were withdrawn from service. Excursion sailings continued on the Clyde with the car ferry *Glen Sannox* from 1978 until 1981, and were revived by the small passenger vessel *Keppel* from 1986 until 1992. The fact that the subsidy granted to Caledonian MacBrayne was for car ferry services rather than for pleasure cruising mitigated against the survival of the latter services.

Eleven of the seventeen MacBrayne vessels – the cargo steamers, tenders/flitboats at such places as Iona, and the surviving non-car ferry vessels – continued to be owned by David MacBrayne Limited for the few years they remained in service.

New ferries have been built at regular intervals over the past forty-one years, the larger ones almost all to one-off designs for particular routes, apart from *Hebrides* and *Clansman*; the intermediate-sized ones comprising the three 'streakers' for upper-Clyde services, *Argyll* and *Bute* on the Wemyss Bay–Rothesay service, and a handful of individual designs. The smaller ones included the eight-strong Island class of landing-craft-type bow-loading vessels, and the four original double-ended 'Lochs' of 1986-1987, which have been followed by a number of similar craft designed for individual routes, and most recently by two hybrid ferries of a similar design with a unique hybrid dual diesel-lithium battery power supply. A handful of miscellaneous vessels complete the story, including those serving the Small Isles and a handful of small motor boats used to tender at ports where there were no piers.

Two routes have been replaced by bridges over the period: the Kyle of Lochalsh to Kyleakin service in 1995, and that from Scalpay to Kyles Scalpay in 1997.

In 2006 the company was restructured. David MacBrayne Ltd was resurrected to become the holding company, CalMac Ferries Ltd was formed to operate the services and Caledonian MacBrayne Assets Ltd to own the ships and charter them to CalMac Ferries Ltd.

This book showcases the CalMac fleet over the past forty-two years at different ports and piers, with some regular calls and some unusual calls.

Chapter 1

THE INHERITED FLEET: CALEDONIAN STEAM PACKET CO. LTD

Queen Mary II

The oldest vessel inherited from the Caledonian Steam Packet (CSP) was the turbine steamer *Queen Mary II*. She had been built in 1933 for Williamson-Buchanan Steamers Ltd by Denny of Dumbarton for the all-the-way trips from Glasgow (Bridge Wharf) to the Clyde Coast. She had continued on these until the closure of the Glasgow berth at the end of the 1969 season. She had then been used on excursion services from Gourock. In 1957 she had been re-boilered her original pair of slender funnels had been replaced by a single large, more modern-looking, one. She had been refurbished internally in 1971.

In 1973, she was sailing to Campbeltown via Brodick on Mondays, Thursdays, Saturdays and Sundays; to Inveraray on Tuesdays; to Brodick and a Holy Isle cruise via the Kyles of Bute on Wednesdays, and Round Bute on Fridays. This was the final year of the long-distance excursions by a turbine steamer, which had been a feature of the Clyde cruising scene since the introduction of the pioneer turbine *King Edward* in 1901.

In 1974, following the withdrawal of *Waverley* at the end of the 1973 season, she offered a cruise Round the Lochs on Tuesdays and Thursdays, with an afternoon portion comprising a cruise to Loch Long and Loch Goil on Tuesdays and a cruise round Bute on Thursdays. An afternoon cruise round Bute was also offered on Fridays and Sundays, and the trip to Arran via the Kyles continued on Wednesdays. 1975 saw a similar programme with a Saturday afternoon Tighnabruaich cruise added. Charters and special sailings from Glasgow in this period operated from Plantation Quay.

Her original name of *Queen Mary* was restored in 1976, a year which saw a return to Glasgow, with an attempt to compete with the preserved *Waverley*. On Sundays and Mondays, she revived her old 11 a.m. departure time from the city, only now sailing from Anderston Quay. On Sundays she sailed to Gourock, Dunoon, Largs, Rothesay, cruising to the Kyles of Bute and Loch Riddon, and on Mondays to the same piers and Tighnabruaich with an hour ashore. Tuesdays, Wednesdays and Thursdays were the same as the previous year and on Saturday she sailed from Gourock to Rothesay, with an afternoon cruise to Carrick Castle. In 1977 on a Sunday, she brought passengers back to Glasgow, as did *Glen Sannox* in 1978 and 1979.

1977 saw advertising for the steamer revive the title of 'Britain's Finest Pleasure Steamer', which she had carried when new in the thirties. In May, she had a week of special cruises for the Queen's Silver Jubilee. Peak season sailings were similar to 1976 but with a few tweaks, including new Saturday sailing from Gourock and Dunoon to Rothesay, Largs and Brodick and returning upriver to Anderston Quay. Her final cruise was an evening showboat cruise from Largs and Rothesay to the Kyles of Bute on 12 September 1977.

That season was her final one in service; she was then laid up in the East India Harbour, Greenock. *Queen Mary II* was sold firstly to Glasgow District Council for preservation as a floating museum, then again in 1980 to be converted in to a floating restaurant in Glasgow. By 1981, no work had been done to her and she was sold for use as a floating restaurant in the Thames. She opened on the Thames Embankment in 1989 after further changes in ownership, with two very thin funnels replacing her single one and her turbines removed. These funnels have had several rather garish paint jobs over the ensuing two decades. In 2009, she was sold for proposed use as a floating restaurant in La Rochelle, France and was towed to Tilbury, where she remains. A further sale at auction in August 2011 has resulted in no progress, with the current owner making no visible efforts to preserve her. There are plans afoot to bring her back to the Clyde as a museum ship, but a lot of money would be needed for such a move. A group called the Friends of Queen Mary has been formed to look into everything possible to endure a future is secured for her. This progressed somewhat in February 2015.

Waverley

The paddle steamer *Waverley* had been built for the London and North Eastern Railway's Clyde services by A. & J. Inglis in 1947. After the nationalisation of the railways she came under CSP control in the following year, although ownership was not transferred from the British Transport Commission to the CSP until 1953. In April 1973 her funnels were painted briefly in an experimental CalMac livery, red with a broad yellow band with the red lion superimposed, and black top. In 1973 she sailed Round Bute on Mondays, Wednesdays, Thursdays and Sundays; Round the Lochs and Firth of Clyde on Tuesdays and Wednesdays; to Tarbert and a cruise on Loch Fyne on Fridays, and an afternoon cruise to Tighnabruaich on Saturdays. She suffered from boiler problems during this season and missed a number of sailings. *Waverley* was withdrawn at the end of the season and was sold for £1 to the Paddle Steamer Preservation Society on 8 August 1974. She re-entered service on 22 May 1975 and since then her career has been well covered elsewhere.

Maid of the Loch

The paddle steamer *Maid of the Loch* was built by A. & J. Inglis, with compound machinery by Rankine & Blackmore of Greenock, in 1953 for the Loch Lomond service. She was built in sections and assembled on the slipway at Balloch. Her funnel was all-over yellow/buff apart from 1975 when a black top was applied to the funnel and, a month into the season, a red band was added for one day and then the remainder of the funnel was painted red. In 1976 she reverted to the original funnel colours. She served on the loch service from Balloch to Balmaha, Rowardennan, Tarbert, Inversnaid and Ardlui until the summer of 1981. Ardlui Pier had been closed in 1971 and Balmaha in 1975, while Luss Pier had been reopened in 1980. *Maid of the Loch* has remained tied up at Balloch Pier ever since, initially becoming more and more derelict under various owners who planned to return her to service, but did nothing. In 1996 she was sold to the Loch Lomond Steamship Co., an organisation supported by the Paddle Steamer

Preservation Society Scottish Branch. Her accommodation has since been restored and she is currently used as a floating café; efforts are in place to obtain funding to return her to operation.

Maid-class Passenger Vessels

All of the four Maid-class passenger vessels dating from 1953 were still in the fleet at the formation of CalMac, but only two sailed for them and received their colours. *Maid of Ashton* was sold in January 1973 for static use on the River Thames in central London, initially as a private club and more recently as a restaurant under the name *Hispaniola* (originally *Hispaniola II*).

Maid of Skelmorlie was sold in April 1973 to Italian owners for service in the Bay of Naples. She entered service in 1976 from Sorrento to Capri under the name *Ala*, having had some of her stern accommodation removed to convert her to a car ferry. From 1997 to 1999 she was chartered to Adriatica Lines for a winter service to the Tremiti Islands in the Adriatic Sea, and in the summer of 2001 was chartered to Di Miao Lines for service from Pozzuoli to the Island of Procida. She later operated from Naples to Sorrento until 2007; she remains in existence, laid up in Naples Harbour having recently been repainted.

Maid of Argyll was the only one of the four to receive the CalMac livery while in her original condition. She operated in 1973 from Wemyss Bay to Rothesay, also replacing *Waverley* on a number of occasions on the round Bute and Tighnabruaich sailings. On 31 August she made her one and only call at Tarbert under the red funnel, replacing *Waverley* while she was out of service for boiler repairs. On 1 March 1974, *Maid of Argyll* was sold to Greek owners, who extended the landing platform to form an upper deck and renamed her *City of Piraeus*, running her on day cruises from Palaeon Phaleron marina, near Piraeus, to the Saronic Islands of Aegina, Poros and Hydra. She was superseded in 1976 by *City of Hydra*, formerly David MacBrayne's *Claymore*, and was then used as a relief vessel and on charters. In 1989 she was moved to Corfu, from where she ran day trips to Parga and Paxos. In 1997 she was ravaged by fire; she was not rebuilt after this, but left to rot and was eventually scrapped.

Maid of Cumbrae had been rebuilt as a car ferry for the Gourock–Dunoon service in 1972. She continued on this route for Caledonian MacBrayne in the summer months, while sailing on a commuter service to Kilcreggan and a once-a-day, peak-hour trip to Dunoon in winter. In February 1976 she called at Coulport on a couple of occasions during a strike by the bus company, and took the workers involved in building the Trident Submarine Base at Coulport there from Kilcreggan. Occasionally, she also saw service replacing *Keppel* on the Largs–Millport route. She was a spare vessel in the summer season from June 1976; her last day in service was 20 May 1978. In August 1978 she was sold to Italian owners, renamed *Hanseatic* for her delivery voyage and placed in service under the name *Noce di Cocco*. As *Noce di Cocco*, she sailed the commuter route from Trieste to Muggia for a short while in 1979 for Navigazione Alto Adriatico. She was then laid up at Trieste and sold for use in the Bay of Naples, renamed as *Capri Express*. By summer 1983, she was on excursions from Capri to Positano with an inflatable swimming pool placed on the car deck. From 1984 she was on the Naples to Sorrento car and ferry service, and in the autumn of 2000 she was running from Pozzuoli to Procida. She was sold for scrapping at Aliaga in Turkey during March 2006.

Arran, Cowal and Bute

Only two of the 1953–1945 trio of hoist-loading car ferries were still on the Firth of Clyde in 1973. *Arran* had been chartered to David MacBrayne Ltd since January 1970 for the West Loch

Tarbert–Islay service. In early 1973 she was converted to be used for stern-loading, with the removal of the hoist and the superstructure aft where the hoist had been, and the fitting of a stern ramp. She was used as a spare vessel after the advent of *Pioneer* in August 1974, covering as relief for ferries off for overhaul in the West Highlands for the remainder of that year. From 1975 she was relief vessel on the Dunoon, Rothesay and Brodick services on the Clyde. In August 1975, a side ramp was added to enable her to serve the linkspan at Dunoon. She continued to provide overhaul relief on the Craignure and Colonsay service and other West Highland services in the winter months. She made an annual sailing from Tiree, Coll and Mingary to Tobermory for the Highland Games there in July. There was an arrangement with the RNAD (Royal Naval Armaments Depot) to provide special sailings from Gourock to Kilcreggan during the construction of the new submarine base at Coulport on Loch Long to convey those working on the project. Following the sale of *Maid of Cumbrae*, she was on the Kilcreggan commuter runs for the RNAD. From 18 May to 17 July 1979 she was on the Small Isles service from Mallaig, awaiting the completion of *Lochmor*. She was withdrawn on 20 July 1979, her final public sailing having been the Tiree to Tobermory games special on the previous day. In 1981 she was sold for static use on the River Liffey in Dublin as a nightclub-cum-restaurant for a company owned by the entertainer Eamonn Andrews, for which she was built up over the former car deck. This closed in 1983 and in November 1986 she was towed to Salford Quays for a similar use until she was broken up in 1993.

Cowal was the last former CSP vessel to retain her former colours, and did not receive the CalMac funnel colours until her overhaul in March/April 1974. *Cowal* served the Wemyss Bay–Rothesay service as the second ferry to Bute in the summer months

of 1974. From 1975 to 1977, she served with *Glen Sannox*, calling at the oil rig construction yard at Ardyne from May 1976. She also did some Wemyss Bay–Innellan crossings to serve the workers at Ardyne. He final run was on 4 June 1977, when work there dried up. In May 1979 she was towed to Greece and was laid up near Piraeus under the name *Med Star* until scrapped in 1984.

Bute started her CalMac career relieving *Columba* on the Oban-Craignure-Lochaline service, then returned to the Wemyss Bay–Rothesay route in February 1973, when she also operated caravan runs from Wemyss Bay to Millport. On 1 October 1974 she was the first CalMac vessel to use the new quay at Ardyne, built for Sir William McAlpine & Co. for the oil-rig construction yard there. She had been doing some extra commuter runs from Wemyss Bay to Innellan, carrying workers for that project since the previous year. She continued to serve Ardyne from both Wemyss Bay and Gourock during the periods she was on the Clyde until 6 May 1977. In April 1975 the horns on her lift were extended to enable her to berth at Armadale, and she served on the summer route from Mallaig to Armadale from then until 1978. In early November 1975, she relieved *Columba* on the Oban to Craignure service and usually relieved on the Clyde routes during the winter months. *Bute* also spent a spell from 16 February to 1 April 1978 relieving *Loch Arkaig* on the Small Isles service from Mallaig.

On 2 October 1977 she called at Canna to load cattle for Oban, and later the same day at Port Askaig for the same purpose. On Sunday 13 August 1978 a temporary ferry door was cut in her starboard ramp and she carried 2,000 lambs from Iona to Oban, where the door was welded shut, and she returned to the Armadale service on the following morning. On 24 September 1978 she visited Craighouse, Jura, on a livestock sailing. She was on the Small Isles service again from 2–21 October 1978, following which she was laid up in the James Watt Dock in Greenock until on 17 June 1980 she sailed for Piraeus under the name *Med Sun*. No work was done on her there and she was scrapped in 1984/5. The reason these two never entered service in Greece was that the project leader died shortly after they arrived there, although *Med Star* was advertised to sail across the Adriatic from Otranto to Igoumenitsa around 1980.

Glen Sannox

Glen Sannox started her CalMac career on the Gourock–Dunoon route. She did not receive her CalMac funnel colours until her overhaul in November 1973. She also relieved on the Arran route, including the busy Easter weekend in 1974. On replacement by *Jupiter* in March 1974 she moved to the Oban–Craignure service from late April to early September of that year, where she was the first ferry to use the new Craignure linkspan. She was on the Wemyss Bay–Ardyne service serving the oil-rig construction yard from 31 October 1974 to 28 October 1976, with occasional sailings on the Rothesay, Dunoon and Brodick services. From November 1976 to late February 1977 she was re-engined at Hall Russell's yard in Aberdeen and her passenger accommodation was remodelled. She then went back to the Gourock–Dunoon route and inaugurated the new linkspan at Wemyss Bay on 20 May 1977. She was then on the Rothesay service until 27 November 1977, when she went onto the Oban to Craignure and Colonsay service until 14 February 1978. In May 1978 she took on *Queen Mary*'s role as a Clyde cruise ship, with a white line round the top of her hull and aircraft-style steps down to the car deck, which now had plastic chairs and tables with sun umbrellas on it. A dance floor was laid on the car deck for the evening showboat cruises. In 1978 and 1979 she did some sailings from Glasgow (Stobcross Quay),

but was not really suited to compete with *Waverley*. Her 1979 programme was:

Sundays: Glasgow to Loch Riddon, sailing in connection with PS *Waverley*.
Mondays: Glasgow to Tighnabruaich, returning to Gourock.
Tuesdays: Gourock to Campbeltown.
Wednesdays: Gourock to Arran via the Kyles.
Thursdays: Round the lochs.
Fridays: Varying cruises, including Tarbert, Rothesay and Round Cumbrae, followed by a Loch Goil cruise and Ayr to Brodick, Largs and Rothesay.
Saturdays: Relief sailings on the Rothesay service with an up-river cruise to Glasgow in the evening.

In 1981 she lost a Strathclyde Regional Council grant, which was won that year by the Firth of Clyde Steam Packet Co., the operators of *Prince Ivanhoe*. The cruise programme was cut back to inter-resort sailings only (Gourock to Dunoon, Rothesay, Largs and Brodick on Mondays and Wednesdays, and to Dunoon, Largs, Rothesay and Tighnabruaich on Tuesdays, Thursdays and Fridays). She returned on the Oban to Craignure and Colonsay run in the winter months, serving there from October to May from 1978 until 5 December 1988. On 6 January 1981 she made her first visit to Coll and Tiree, returning via Craignure; from mid-January to March of that year she was on the Kennacraig–Islay service, spending odd spells there in the ensuing years. In June 1981 she spent a spell relieving *Columba* on her sailings from Oban to Coll and Tiree, to Colonsay and to Iona, for which purpose a ferry door was cut near her stern, although no landings were possible at Iona while she was on this roster.

In 1982 the Clyde cruising programme was abandoned entirely until the advent of the cruises by *Keppel* in 1986. In 1982 she spent long spells laid up in the James Watt Dock, and spent much of that summer on the Wemyss Bay–Rothesay run, as *Saturn* had engine problems. In 1983 she had two-and-a-half weeks on the Brodick service from the end of July to the beginning of August, but was laid up for most of the remainder of the summer. The summer of 1984 saw a number of spells relieving on the Islay service; this pattern of winter sailings to Craignure and Colonsay, with summers laid up at Greenock or with relief sailings to Rothesay, Brodick and Islay as required, continued. On 9 May 1987 she was on a Clyde River Steamer Club excursion from Gourock to Troon and Stranraer to mark her 30th anniversary. On 31 July and 1 August of that year, she relieved *Columba* and sailed from Oban to Coll and Tiree and to Colonsay. On 31 August she had a special excursion from Gourock to Ardrishaig in connection with a special train from England. She spent 1989 on relief sailings on the Islay, Craignure or Colonsay and Brodick routes, punctuated by spells laid up at Greenock. She made her final sailing for the company, a charter for Govan Shipbuilders from Govan to Rothesay, on 10 June. She was sold to Greek owners and left Greenock for Piraeus on 24 July 1989 under the name *Knooz*. A new aft superstructure was added in Greece and she operated in the Red Sea pilgrim trade, being renamed *Nadia*, then *Al Marwah* in 1991 and *Al Bismalah I* in 1994. She ran aground south of Jeddah in 2000 and is apparently still lying there, rotting. She was arguably the finest ferry ever to operate for CalMac.

Kyleakin and *Coruisk*, *Isle of Cumbrae*, *Portree* and *Broadford*

The former Kyle–Kyleakin ferries, *Kyleakin* (1960) and *Coruisk* (1969), had been moved to a new crossing from Largs to Cumbrae slip in 1972. The former turntable-ferry *Kyleakin* was converted to bow-loading and renamed *Largs,* while *Coruisk* was converted

from side-loading to bow-loading. From the advert of *Isle of Cumbrae* in 1977, *Largs* acted as a spare vessel there mainly in the summer months, and also relieved the larger ferry for overhaul. She was sold to Ardmaleish Shipyard at Rothesay in November 1983 and laid up until sold to South Yemen owners in 1987 – she was taken there as deck cargo on a Dutch freighter.

Coruisk had inaugurated the new route from Largs to Cumbrae Slip on 11 March 1972. Following the arrival of *Isle of Cumbrae* in 1977, she was used as a relief vessel at Largs, Colintraive, Iona, Mingary and at Scalpay and spent much of her time as the spare ferry on the Kyle–Kyleakin crossing. From 1984 she was the regular replacement vessel at Largs during *Isle of Cumbrae*'s overhaul periods. She was sold in September 1986 to Euroyachts, who sold her on to an owner in Penzance. She was later renamed *Mayo III*. In 1988 she was sold to Lampogas S. p. A and, renamed *Lampomare Uno*, used to carry gas tankers and other hazardous cargos from Piombins to Portoferraio on the island of Elba, being painted yellow all over. She was re-engined in 1993 and was still in service until the early years of the present century. In 2005 she was sold to Geosystem srl and renamed *Seageo*, and was still in existence in 2011.

Two more former Kyle to Kyleakin ferries had been moved south for the Colintraive to Rhubodach service. *Portree* of 1965 had been converted to bow-loading in 1970 and was transferred to the Colintraive–Rhubodach service in May of that year, where she served until 1986. *Broadford* of 1967 had been converted to bow-loading in 1971 and moved to the Colintraive–Rhubodach service in June of that year. Both were sold in November 1987 to an owner at Sandbank to carry supplies to the US Navy ships in the Holy Loch. *Broadford* was sold on to Welsh owners in 1988 and renamed *Boreford*. In the early years of the new millennium she came back to the Clyde for use as a workboat under the name of *Broadford Bay*, with her ramp removed, and was scrapped around 2005.

Keppel

British Railways' former Tilbury–Gravesend passenger-ferry *Rose* (1961) had been transferred to the CSP in 1966 for the Largs–Millport passenger service and renamed *Keppel*. She introduced Voith-Schneider propulsion to the Clyde fleet and had rather basic passenger accommodation, along with a tall, thin funnel-cum-mast which was replaced by a larger one that was wide enough for the addition of a lion to it, after a year or two. She had sailed year-round until the 1970/71 winter. In June 1986, the Millport passenger service was withdrawn and *Keppel* became the Clyde cruise vessel. Cruises were mainly in the nearer reaches of the Firth with destinations including Carrick Castle and Tighnabruaich. She was noted for her lack of speed and was not really a success as a cruise vessel. She was withdrawn in 1993 and sold to a Greenock owner who renamed her *Clyde Rose*, intending to use her on charters and special sailings, for example to the Millport illuminations. She was laid up after one season and was sold to owners in Malta in 1995, where she regained the name *Keppel* and still offers cruises there under the flag of Hornblower Cruises.

Caledonia

The car ferry *Caledonia*, previously *Stena Baltica*, had entered service on the Ardrossan–Brodick service in 1970 and was, at the time of the formation of Caledonian MacBrayne, their only ferry with both bow and stern loading. Her vehicle deck was too small, her passenger accommodation was rather basic and a winter-passenger certificate of 132 led to complaints from Arran residents. In 1976 she was transferred to the Oban–Craignure service in the summer months. From April 1984 she saw littler

service on the Arran run, following the advent of *Isle of Arran*. On 28 June 1986, unusually, she made a commercial vehicle crossing from Oban to Lochboisdale. Her 1986 Oban season was extended until November. On 26 April 1987 she made her one and only visit to Tobermory with a special public sailing from Oban for the Mull Music Festival. She was withdrawn from service on 21 October 1987 and sold that December to an owner in Broughty Ferry for a proposed conversion to a floating restaurant. However, no work was done on her and she was sold a year later for use in the Gulf of Naples, where she ran under the name *Heidi* from Pozzuoli to Ischia until 2004 when she was laid up at Naples. She sank at her moorings there on 10 July 2005 and was raised and sold for scrapping at Aliaga in Turkey.

Queen Mary II berthed at Tighnabruaich late in her CalMac career.

Queen Mary arriving at Gourock in 1976.

A deck view on *Queen Mary*.

Queen Mary berthed at Tighnabruaich in 1976.

Restaurant Ship *Queen Mary* in London, 1997.

Above left: *Waverley* off Dunoon in CalMac colours in 1973.

Right: *Waverley* at Gourock in 1973 from *Queen Mary II*. In both photographs on the page the CSP flag is being flown. The combined flag was not introduced until July 1973.

Maid of Cumbrae arriving at Gourock while *Maid of Argyll* lies at the wires, 1973.

Above: The cover of a brochure for the Saronic Islands cruises by *City of Piraeus*, ex *Maid of Argyll*.

Above left: Cowal at Rothesay. Note the Buggy used to tow the trailers onto the car ramp, and the primitive wooden gangway compared to those of today.

Above right: The demolition of *Med Sun*, ex *Bute*, in Greece. (A. Scrimali)

Right: Arran arriving at Oban, 1975 in her rebuilt condition post-1973.

Opposite page, above left: Maid of Cumbrae in mid-Firth.

Opposite page, above right: Maid of Cumbrae as *Noce di Cocco* at Trieste, April 1979 (Dr G. Spazapan).

Opposite page, left: Cowal off Toward in CalMac colours.

Above left: Arran at Dublin as a night club, 1982.

Above right: Arran arriving at Gourock with *Countess of Kempock* at the pier.

Left: Arran at Oban Railway Pier, May 1978.

Above left: Glen Sannox departing from Oban in 1974.

Above right: Glen Sannox departing from Largs in 1979. Note the coloured umbrellas in the car deck.

Right: Glen Sannox and the two white stripes of the cruising livery on the hull at Port Ellen at *Lochiel*'s former berth on the Islay service, seen with *Waverley*, 23 April 1982.

Above left: Glen Sannox at Oban with the company name on her hull, 1 April 1988, taken from *Columba* which has arrived on a special cruise from Largs via Tarbert.

Above right: Glen Sannox undergoing conversion in a dry dock in Perama, Greece under the name *Knooz*.

Left: Broadford turns having just left Rhubodach.

Above left: *Coruisk* at Largs slipway, 1975.

Above right: *Largs* (ex *Kyleakin*) approaching Largs slipway.

Right: *Broadford* and *Portree* off Colintraive.

Above left: Keppel arriving at Millport, 1975.

Above right: Keppel at the CalMac HQ at Gourock, 1991, with the company name now on the hull.

Left: Caledonia in the James Watt Dock, 1986, reflecting on her CalMac career.

Chapter 2

THE INHERITED FLEET: EX DAVID MacBRAYNE VESSELS

King George V
The turbine steamer *King George V* had been built in 1926 by Denny of Dumbarton for Turbine Steamers Ltd for the Greenock to Inverary service. She had been purchased by David MacBrayne Ltd in October 1935 and had been on the Sacred Isle cruise from Oban to Staffa and Iona ever since, with the exception of the war years, a season on the Ardrishaig Mail service in 1946 and on occasional short spells relieving there. In 1973 and 1974 she continued on the route under the new CalMac colours, and in 1974 her brown ventilators were repainted in pale blue. She sailed from mid-May to mid-September each year. On 3 August 1973, it was announced that she was to go to the Ullapool–Stornoway service to replace the broken-down *Clansman*, but the Department of Transport refused her a passenger certificate for the service. In addition to the sacred isle cruise, she sailed from Fort William and Oban to Iona on Wednesdays, and on Fridays in 1973 she made two return trips from Oban to Fort William. On Fridays in 1974 she sailed a cruise from Fort William and Oban to the Isles of the Sea and Corryvreckan Whirlpool. In 1974 her Oban sailings were from the Railway Pier rather than the North Pier. She was withdrawn after the 1974 season and was sold in 1975 for a proposed conversion to a floating restaurant, but languished in the Mount Stuart Dry Dock at Cardiff until gutted by fire on 26 August 1981, following which she was scrapped. The much lamented KGV is fondly remembered today in and around Oban.

Lochnell
The motor-launch *Lochnell*, built in 1941 and purchased in 1947, continued on the Tobermory–Mingary service in the CalMac era. In addition to her thrice-daily service on the route, she offered some afternoon cruises from Tobermory to Ardnamurchan Point and Loch Sunart until 1975, and from 1976 a fourth-daily crossing was offered in the summer months. She was withdrawn on 11 October 1980 and her only duty then was to tender to the Coll and Tiree ferry on three days a week till the end of the year. She was then laid up at Shandon and sold on 10 June 1981. She was laid up for a long time at Renfrew, and in 1990 a saloon was added aft and she offered cruises on

Loch Leven from Ballachulish slate quarries under the name *Loch Nell*. This continued in 1991 under the ownership of the Forth & Clyde Tea Company. In 1992 she was sold to the new Isles of Glencoe Hotel, but did not operate for them. She was then mainly used as a private yacht on the Clyde. She was moved to Shepperton, on the Thames, in November 2009 for use as a houseboat, and then towed to Faversham and taken out of the water for restoration in 2011. In July 2012 she was offered for sale on eBay for £4,000 but there were no bidders.

Loch Seaforth

Loch Seaforth had been built in 1948, also by Dennys, for the Mallaig and Kyle of Lochalsh to Stornoway mail service and, after being replaced by the car-ferry *Clansman* in 1972, had been moved to the Inner Isles service from Oban to Tobermory, Coll, Tireee, Castlebay and Lochboisdale. On 2 January 1973 she added a thrice-weekly service for Oban–Colonsay to her duties. Around 6 a.m. on 22 March 1973 she hit a rock in the Sound of Gunna between Coll and Tiree and was holed in the engine room. The passengers and crew, including chairman Moris Little and managing director John Whittle, took to the lifeboats. The one containing the crew made for the shore and other lifeboat made straight for the pier. The crew then returned to the ship, and with the assistance of a tug moved her to Tiree Pier. She sank and settled on the bottom there on the following day. On 21 May she was raised by the floating crane *Magnus III* and was towed to Troon a couple of days later and broken up there.

Lochdunvegan and Loch Carron

The cargo vessel *Lochdunvegan* (1949) was still in service in 1973 on the cargo route, which included Stornoway and Kyle of Lochalsh. On most Saturdays in July and August she was used to carry cars from Tiree to Oban as a back-up to *Claymore*. She was sold on 2 November 1973 to Greek owners.

Loch Carron (1951) was on the Outer Isles cargo service, and her roster included *Lochdunvegan's* calls from 1 October 1973; from then on she sailed every ten days until she was withdrawn on 7 November 1976. She was sold to Greek owners on 28 April 1977 and sailed for Greece under the name *Georgios X* on 7 May. She was renamed a further four times, latterly under the Honduras flag, and is believed to have been broken up in the 1990s.

Claymore

The 1955 Inner Isles mail vessel *Claymore*, another Denny product, began the new era laid up in the East India Harbour, Greenock. She was hurriedly reactivated and returned to the route on 22 March after the *Loch Seaforth* was wrecked. This now included a thrice-weekly service sailing from Oban to Colonsay, berthing overnight there on Mondays and Thursdays. There was now, in the summer timetable period, only a once-weekly sailing to Castlebay and Barra; sailings to Tobermory, Coll and Tiree on Mondays, Tuesdays, and Fridays; and twice on Saturdays, with departures from Oban at 1:30 a.m. and 1 p.m. The Tuesday and Friday sailings also called at Craignure and Lochaline. The red ferry-boat *Iona* was used at Tiree until the wreck of *Loch Seaforth* was cleared from the pier. From summer 1974, the Castlebay and Lochboisdale sailings were operated by *Iona*. *Claymore* concentrated on the Coll and Tiree service, which was now offered daily with the calls at Craignure not scheduled, and with a double Saturday service from 25 May to 14 September. She was laid up after her final Coll and Tiree sailing on 5 October 1974, and returned to the Coll and Tiree service from 25 to 29 October 1975, following which she continued on the Colonsay service until 9 November, replacing *Columba*, which had taken over the Coll and Tiree service.

She was sold in April 1976, leaving for Piraeus on 10 May under the name *City of Andros* to undergo a major rebuild for service as a day-cruise vessel in Greek waters. She emerged as *City of Hydra* after an extensive rebuild and the addition of a small swimming pool, operating from Palaeon Phaleron, near Piraeus, to the Saronic Islands until she laid up in 1993. She spent several years laid up until she sank at her moorings in 2000.

Loch Toscaig

The former motor fishing vessel *Loch Toscaig* (1949) started her CalMac career on the Oban to Lismore service. On 12 September 1973 she had a major engine breakdown; her engine was removed and she was towed to the Crinan Canal by *Morvern* on 2 December, and then by *Lochnell* from Ardrishaig to Shandon on 22 December, where she received a reconditioned engine and a new crankshaft. She re-entered service going onto the Tobermory–Mingary route on 15 March 1974. She was relieved by *Lochnell* on 21 May and was a spare vessel, based at Lochaline, Tobermory and Oban, for the remainder of the year. On 15 November she was moved to Shandon and was put up for sale. She was sold for private use in October 1975 and later offered fishing trips from Gourock.

MacBrayne 'Red Boats'

A number of former MacBrayne 'Red Boats' were operated by CalMac. *Ulva* (1956) was used on the Fionnphort–Iona service and tendered *King George V*, and later *Columba*, at Iona. She was moved to Eigg in 1980 after the island-class ferry *Morvern* had taken over the Iona service and served as a flitboat there until December 2000, by which time she was the last of the 'Red Boats'. She was sold in March 2001 to a Fort William buyer who was only interested in her engine.

Iona (1962) served at Iona and also at Tiree when the pier was blocked by the sunken *Loch Seaforth*. She also served at Tobermory, when the pier was being rebuilt in the mid-eighties, and at Eigg. Whilst undergoing her annual overhaul in February 1988, she was found to be riddled with woodworm and was demolished forthwith.

Eigg (1923), used as a flitboat at Eigg, was withdrawn in September 1974 and scrapped in 1978.

Loch Arkaig

Loch Arkaig, the rebuilt wooden-hulled, former in-shore minesweeper, continued on the combined Small Isles and Portree roster, which she maintained until March 1975. From then on she was purely on the Small Isles run, with additional Mallaig–Kyle of Lochalsh runs in the summer months. In 1973 she offered some evening cruises from Portree to Raasay. On occasion, she would carry a solitary car perched on the top of her wheelhouse on the scheduled service for Raasay. In 1977 she started offering some afternoon cruises to Loch Duich and off Eilean Donan Castle from Kyle; in 1978 afternoon cruises were given to Portree and to Loch Alsh. On 28 March 1979 she sank in Mallaig harbour and was sold in October of that year for conversion to a yacht. She was again sold to Arab owners and was reported to have sunk off the Spanish Coast near Cadiz in October 1985.

Hebrides, Clansman and Columba

Two of the 1964 trio of hoist-loading car ferries, *Hebrides* and *Columba*, continued on their previous routes in 1973, respectively the Uig Triangle and from Oban to Craignure. *Clansman* started the year under conversion to a drive-through ferry with a bow visor and stern doors. She was also lengthened by 35 feet, the forward part of her superstructure being raised by 3 feet and the aft by 5 feet. On 29 June she re-entered service from Ullapool to Stornoway, serving there until replaced by *Suilven* on 28 August 1974. She replaced *Glen Sannox* on the Oban–Craignure service for a month from 2 September 1974. In the summer of 1975 she spent spells replacing *Suilven* and the Orkney ferry *St Ola* for overhaul. On 24 April 1976 she started on the Ardrossan–Brodick summer service; from March to early October replacing *Caledonia* and continuing her previous pattern of relief sailings in the winter months, from Ullapool to Stornoway and from Scrabster to Stromness. She continued on this routine until 17 March 1984 when she was taken out of service with an engine failure.

She was laid up and was sold in August that year to Torbay Seaways for a proposed service from Torquay to the Channel Islands. Planning permission was refused for a linkspan at Torquay and she was sold on to a Maltese owner, who renamed her *Tamira*. She was then again sold and renamed *Al Hussein* and chartered for operation in the Red Sea. In 1986 she was yet again sold and renamed *Al Rasheed*, operating across the Red Sea from Jeddah to Massaua. In 2002 she was reported as having being abandoned off the coast of Sudan, where she can still be seen on Google Earth at co-ordinates 19 22′ 35.87″ N, 37 18′ 56.11″ E.

Hebrides continued on the Uig–Tarbet–Lochmaddy service until 1985. On 2 and 3 January 1973 she was on the Ardrossan–Brodick service, assisting *Caledonia*, and on 1 July of that year she made a special commercial-vehicle sailing from Ullapool to Stornoway, replacing the broken-down *Clansman*. On 30 March 1975, she made one crossing with cars from Brodick to Largs, and one from Brodick to Gourock. In her 1975 overhaul she received a second radar scanner on a new platform on the foremast, below the existing one, a feature that helps to distinguish her from *Columba* in photographs.

On the evening of 14 February 1976, she made a livestock sailing from Tiree to Oban; on the evenings of 25 February 1976 and 19 February 1977 she made livestock sailings from Lochmaddy to Oban; on 28 April 1977, she took livestock from Lochboisdale and Castlebay to Oban, and again on 30 April 1977 from Colonsay to Oban. On 20 August 1978, she conveyed livestock from Tiree to Oban. 10 December 1978 saw another Lochboisdale to Oban livestock sailing, and there was another on 9 December 1979 from Lochboisdale, Castlebay and Coll to Oban. On 23 January 1980, she replaced the broken down *Columba* on a Coll–Oban sailing. On 4 June 1981 she lost a rudder and was towed to Greenock for a replacement to be fitted. It was 1 July 1981 when she returned to service, having had the replacement manufactured and fitted. She had been replaced by *Columba*, and, on her way north, took *Columba*'s sailings out of Oban to Iona, to Tobermory, Coll and Tiree, and to Colonsay for three days. She was on the Ardrossan–Brodick service again from 4 to 6 March 1982. From 1982 onwards she was laid up in Greenock from mid-January (February in 1985) to mid-March (1982) or mid-April.

She made her final sailings on 13 November 1985 and was sold to Torbay Seaways for the service they had planned for *Clansman* the previous year, from Torquay to the Channel

Islands. She served this as *Devoniun* until 1994 when she was sold to a Greek, Liberian-registered operator, and operated from Bari and Brindisi to the Albanian ports of Vlore and Durres under the name *Illyria* for Illiria Lines. In 1998, she may have crossed the Atlantic to run from St Vincent to the Grenadines or she may have been reregistered in a company with that flag, and was laid up in Eleusis Bay, Greece in October 1999. She was sold for breaking up at Alang, India in 2003.

The third of the 1964 trio, *Columba*, started her CalMac career in 1973, relieving other ferries in the network for overhaul. On 30 April she started her summer service on the Mallaig–Armadale route, with overnight sailings to Lochboisdale and Castlebay, she also served on the Armadale route in the summer of 1974 with no Outer Isles sailings.

In 1975 she started a new summer routine, based at Oban and replacing *King George V* with two weekly sailings to Staffa and Iona, thrice-weekly to Colonsay, four weekly sailings to Lochaline, Tobermory, Coll and Tiree, and one sailing directly to Tiree and calling at Coll on the homeward journey. These islands now had their own service from Oban, having previously been served by the Castlebay and Lochboisdale inner-islands vessel. These sailings were combined to make mini-cruises using the passenger cabins on board. She continued these sailings every summer until 1988. In 1975, the *Iona* sailings were via the south of Mull in both directions and extended to a cruise round Staffa on the outward voyage, but were round Mull from 1976 onwards. At the end of September, after the end of her cruise season, she continued on Colonsay sailings for a further month. She was initially on the Craignure and Colonsay roster in the winter months, also relieving on the Uig Triangle until 1986 from late January to March (mid-April from 1982 onwards) each year, and from Oban to Castlebay and Lochboisdale and Coll and Tiree services. She also made a variety of spring and autumn livestock sailings including calls at Bruichladdich, Islay in April 1978.

The beginning of the mini-cruise season in early May saw a specially advertised passenger-carrying positioning trip from Gourock to Oban in 1978 and 1979. In 1979 this was extended by a cruise to St Kilda, where a select few were landed. The St Kilda sailing was repeated in 1980, but just from Oban, with a call at Castlebay in both directions. From 27 December 1980 until 5 January 1981, she was on the Ardrossan–Brodick service. On her summer cruise programme from 1982 she sailed from Oban Railway Pier rather than North Pier. On 12 May 1983 she was on charter to Howard Doris for a VIP trip, with passengers including HRH Prince Charles, from Strome Ferry to the Kishorn oil-rig construction yard. The calls at Tobermory ceased on 28 May 1983 due to the poor condition of the pier, and the Lochaline calls were not made after the 1986 summer. Following the withdrawal of *Hebrides*, she took on the Uig Triangle service on 14 November 1985; she maintained this until she was replaced by *Hebridean Isles* on 8 May of the following year with a couple of emergency trips to the Clyde for repairs in February and April. Another mini-cruise to St Kilda was advertised on 3 May 1987, but was cancelled because of adverse weather and eventually took place on 29 August. On 1 April 1988 she undertook a special trip from Largs via Tarbert to Oban. Her final sailing for the company was on 30 September 1988.

She was then sold to Hebridean Princess Cruises and renamed *Hebridean Princess*. Since 1989 she has been active in the luxury cruise market, having been remodelled to resemble a country house hotel. In the 1993/1994 winter, her hoist was removed and cabins installed in the former car deck. Her sailings have been mainly in the Clyde and West Highlands and Islands, with occasional forays to the Norwegian fjords and to the coast of Normandy and Brittany, and with one or two visits to London. In July 2006 and July 2010 she was chartered by Her Majesty Queen Elizabeth II for use as a royal yacht. In June 2009 she was taken over by All Leisure Ltd, owners of Swan Hellenic Cruises and Voyages of Discovery, but has continued operating as previously.

Iona

Iona, built in 1970 by Ailsa at Troon, started her CalMac career on the Mallaig–Kyle–Stornoway service in its dying days. This was replaced by a twice-daily Ullapool to Stornoway service on 26 March 1973. On 26 June she broke down, was replaced by the rebuilt *Clansman* three days later and moved to Oban for the Craignure service on 12 July. She moved to the Clyde at the end of October for a short spell on the Gourock–Dunoon service, and returned to the Mull route with twice-weekly Colonsay sailings in mid-December. On 29 April 1974 she opened the new, direct Oban–Castlebay–Lochboisdale service. In winter 1974/75 she added Coll and Tiree calls to her sailings. In February 1975 she had a major rebuild at the Robb Caledon yard at Leith. A new deckhouse with eight cabins was added to the upper deck and the small funnel was removed. The exhaust uptakes were lengthened by six feet and painted as funnels and the original small, toy-like dummy funnel was removed.

Allan Campbell MacLean, writing in the West Highland Free Press on 6 June 1975, was less than complimentary to *Iona*:

The day of the family amphibious saloon has not yet come. We are spared the sight of tourists – yachting caps at a jaunty angle – driving off the end of the pier at Ullapool and setting

course for Stornoway. The seaways are happily free of the omnivorous car, which is devouring all that is best in the urban environment, and increasingly fouling the countryside.

Vandals – disguised as your friendly local councillor – connive in the urban destruction by sanctioning the construction of multi-storied car parks in town centres. These monstrous concrete mausoleums – invariably disfiguring the centre, no matter how small and attractive the town – only succeed in adding to the already chaotic traffic congestion. Henry Ford thought he was liberating the peasants when his mass-produced Model T rolled off the first primitive assembly lines. In fact, he was shackling Western man in servitude to the car. Even naval architects have fallen under its baleful influence, as anyone who has travelled aboard the Iona can testify.

A comparatively recent addition to the CalMac fleet, the Iona is a floating car-park, expressly designed for the comfort and convenience of the automobile. In the eyes of her designer, human freight was clearly a secondary – if not a minor – consideration. Seating and promenade space on deck is virtually non-existent. The arrangement in what is laughingly labelled the observation lounge is of so uncompromisingly bleak a nature that it might have been lifted straight from a Victorian House of Correction. In keeping with the reformatory atmosphere, on the day I crossed from Tiree to Oban aboard the Iona the shutters remained firmly in place on the for'ard windows. A drab expanse of shuttered windows does little to enhance a long sea journey. Of course it may have been part of a none too subtle plot to drive the disgruntled passenger to the bar.

The smoke-room/bar, deep in the bowels of the ship, has all the charm, colour and gaiety and warmth of a public lavatory. On the other hand, it could have been a faithful replica of the traditional old-tyme Glasgow drinking den.

What a joy then to board an older vessel, the Hebrides, and travel in comfort to Tarbert by way of Lochmaddy. The Hebrides is everything that the Iona is not. There is every facility for the human passenger – on deck and below deck – and the relaxed, pleasant service that one remembers from earlier days when CalMac was simply MacBrayne.

Given such an admirably equipped and well-run vessel, it is curious that CalMac should go to such extraordinary lengths to confuse the travelling public as to her whereabouts on any given day. The essence of a good timetable, designed to cultivate custom, is a simple regularity. 'Simple' is the last word that could be used to describe the incredibly complicated timetable of the Hebrides. I defy anyone to commit it to memory, even after an intensive study.

Obviously, this convoluted schedule was devised by a malevolent dwarf with a grudge against humanity and a mad passion for cars. He wants the Hebrides withdrawn from service and replaced by an austere floating car-park, and has hit upon a beautifully simple solution – a timetable of such baffling complexity that CalMac returns on the Uig–Tarbert–Lochmaddy run will suffer such a drastic fall that the service will be discontinued.

CalMac should scrap the existing schedule and replace it with a sensible timetable. As for the malevolent dwarf, I have the perfect solution for him. He should be given a CalMac cardboard cup and plastic knife, and banished to the smoke-room of the Iona.

She continued on the Barra/Boisdale service until the end of 1978 when she was replaced by *Claymore*. She was moved on 15 February 1979, following her refit, to the Islay route which was now running from Kennacraig rather than from West Loch Tarbert. In October each year from 1980 until 1988, with the exception of 1983, in December 1980, from February to mid-April 1982, in the second half of August and the first week in September 1983, and in June 1986 she replaced *Claymore* for overhaul or repairs for up to a month on each occasion on the Oban to Castlebay and Lochboisdale service.

For the first half of April 1982 she ran three days a week on the Craignure service and three days a week to Lochboisdale. She had a couple of days relieving on the Arran service in February 1984, twelve days in April 1986 and a month each from 20 October 1986, 12 October 1987, and 17 October 1988 on the Uig Triangle. She suffered frequently from gearbox problems until a new gearbox was fitted in March 1987. Her first spell on the Armadale service was from 20 to 25 July 1987.

She continued on the Islay route until June 1989, when she was again replaced by *Claymore* and moved to the Mallaig–Armadale route in summer, with a weekly Mallaig to Castlebay sailing on Sundays. She continued to provide relief sailings on other routes in the winter months, mainly to Islay, and also on the Uig Triangle and ran services out of Oban and Ardrossan to Arran in February from 1991 to 1993. In July 1988, her hoist failed and she returned to the Islay service for a month. For five weeks in June and July 1990, she was back on the Islay service after her bow-thrust unit failed and had to be sent to Holland for repairs. In the summer months from 1991 to 1993 she offered a Sunday sailing from Mallaig and Armadale to Tobermory, Coll and Tiree. On 12 September 1993 she made her first call at the newly extended pier at Canna, on a livestock sailing, calling again on 3 October.

In April 1994, linkspans were finally opened at Mallaig and Armadale. In summer from 1994 to 1996 a twice-weekly evening and overnight Mallaig to Castlebay and Lochboisdale service was operated. From 11 to 21 March 1996 she was on the Dunoon and Rothesay services after *Juno* had a major breakdown and *Pioneer* was relieving on the Small Isles run. On 6 May 1996 she sailed from Mallaig to Lochmaddy to take an overflow of cars to Tarbert during the Western Isles Challenge Race, and on 7 September 1996 made a Tarbert to Uig sailing as back-up to *Hebridean Isles* after *Isle of Lewis* had broken down. In March 1997 she relieved on the Small Isles run from Mallaig for the first, and only, time.

Summer 1997 saw her on a weekly sailing from Mallaig to Coll and Tiree and a weekly Mallaig to Castlebay and Lochboisdale sailing. Special steamer-enthusiast sailings were made on 7 April 1990 from Gourock and Largs to Brodick and Ardrishaig, and on 3 April 1993 from Gourock to Wemyss Bay, Tighnabruaich and Tarbert, returning via Rothesay and Dunoon. In April 1992 she ran a series of charters for German tourists from Mallaig to Kyle of Lochalsh. A passenger trip was offered on 30 March 1996 from Gourock and Dunoon to Campbeltown and Kennacraig. Her final CalMac sailing was on 25 October 1997 from Armadale to Mallaig.

She was sold to Pentland Ferries, by whom she was renamed *Pentalina B* and laid up at St Margaret's Hope because the terminal at Gills Bay were still under construction. She was chartered back to CalMac in 1998 after *Isle of Lewis* had a major breakdown and *Isle of Mull* had been sent to Stornoway to relieve her. She served on the Oban–Craignure route from 26 April to 14 May. She finally entered service for Pentland Ferries on 3 May 2001, although she could only carry twelve passengers in the winter months. From January 2004 she was laid up in the winter months. From the end of November 2006 she was chartered to Farmers Ferry to carry cattle from Dover to Dunkirk, but this was interrupted in August 2007 by restrictions following an outbreak of foot and mouth disease. She sailed for a brief period in early September 2007 from Ipswich as repairs were being made to her berth at Dover. She returned to the Pentland Firth crossing from 21 November 2007 to 6 January 2008. From 10 to 27 December 2008 she was chartered to CalMac again for the freight service to Stornoway.

The early part of 2009 saw only occasional sailings from Ipswich and Dover to Dunkirk, with much time spent laid up at the French port. She was chartered to CalMac again from 2 to 17 April 2009 for the Kennacraig–Port Askaig service, mainly with freight traffic. She was sold in January 2010 to owners in the Cape Verde Islands, where she operated carrying machinery and heavy loads between the islands until she ran aground in the bay of Móia-Moia on the island of Santiago in June 2013 whilst en route from the island of Boa Vista to Praia. After a week or two, a causeway with a basic roadway was constructed to enable the vehicles on board to disembark, and it was reported uncertain if she would be salvaged.

The final ferry to enter service for David MacBrayne Ltd before the 1973 merger to form Caledonian MacBrayne was the island-class vessel *Kilbrannan* in 1972. Her history is dealt with in chapter five.

King George V crosses Oban Bay from the Railway Pier to the North Pier, summer 1973.

Above: Lochnell in Cardwell Bay long after she had left the CalMac fleet.

Right: King George V in the Mount Stuart Dry Dock, Cardiff, January 1978, where she was destroyed by fire there years later.

Above left: *Lochnell* at Ballachulish in August 1990, when she was doing cruises on Loch Leven.

Above right: Cargo vessel *Loch Carron* in the Sound of Mull, 1974.

Left: Cargo vessel *Loch Carron* at Coll. (Gordon Law)

Above left: Lismore ferry *Loch Toscaig* at Oban North Pier, September 1969, with a classic MacBrayne coach in the background.

Above right: The 1955 *Claymore* at Oban Railway Pier.

Right: *Claymore* at Tiree with Tiree Pipe band coming down the pier, 1973.

1 day cruise
jour de croisière
tag kreuzfahrt

3 islands
iles
inseln

Hydra Poros Aegina

T.M.V CITY OF HYDRA

K

cycladic cruises s.a

Above left: Claymore as *City of Hydra*, off Hydra, Greece 1978.

Above right: Loch Arkaig at Mallaig, 1973 with *Columba*.

Left: An advertising card for *City of Hydra's* Saronic Islands cruises.

Above: The former *Hebrides* as *Illyria* in a Mediterranean port.

Right: Hebrides at Gourock, April 1981.

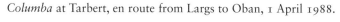

Columba at Tarbert, en route from Largs to Oban, 1 April 1988.

A large crowd of steamer enthusiasts on the aft deck of *Columba* on a special positioning sailing from the Clyde to Oban.

Right: The much travelled *Hebridean Princess* (ex *Columba*) at Oban North Pier, 1997.

Clansman at sea, 1982.

Clansman, as converted to a drive-through car ferry, passes Inverkip Power Station, January 1976.

Left: The 'wee red boat' *Eigg* at her namesake island, 1973.

Above: Flitboat *Ulva* at the jetty at Eigg.

Above left: Ulva approaching *Lochmor* off Eigg.

Above right: Iona in original condition approaching Craignure prior to 1975. Her original funnel was too small to have a CalMac lion attached.

Right: Iona departing from Mallaig in summer 1997, with Eastern European fish factory ships in the left background.

Iona at Rothesay on 3 April 1993 on a special enthusiast cruise.

Iona at Tighnabruaich on the same day.

Left: Iona at Tarbert, Loch Fyne on the same cruise.

Right: Pentalina B (ex *Iona*) at Oban on 3 May 1998 on charter to CalMac.

Chapter 3

INTERMEDIATE-SIZE FERRIES

In the mid-seventies, three ferries were built which would be the mainstay of the upper-Clyde services for the next thirty years and more: *Jupiter* and *Juno* (1974) for the Gourock–Dunoon service, and *Saturn* (1978) for the Wemyss Bay–Rothesay route. The first two were built by James Lamont & Co. Ltd. at Port Glasgow, and the third by Ailsa Shipbuilding at Troon. All had an open-car deck aft, a stern ramp and two side-ramps, and two levels of enclosed passenger accommodation. The Lamont-built ships had A-shaped masts rising from the funnels and *Saturn* had a mast at the rear of her superstructure. *Juno* and *Jupiter* started life with the legend 'GOUROCK DUNOON FERRY' painted on the hull, where *Saturn* had 'ROTHESAY FERRY'. *Saturn*'s was removed in November 1982, *Jupiter*'s in January 1983 and *Juno*'s in December 1984. All three had the words 'Caledonian MacBrayne' painted on the hull in 1985. The three ferries were collectively known as 'Streakers' and, in place of propellers, had two Voith-Schneider units fore and aft, which enabled them to make a 360-degree turn when necessary. They were the last CalMac ships to be built with wooden decks.

Jupiter, *Juno* and *Saturn*

Jupiter was launched on 25 November 1973, two days after CalMac decided to gift *Waverley* to the Paddle Steamer Preservation Society, and entered service on 19 March 1974 from Gourock to Dunoon, followed by *Juno* on 2 December 1974. They also incorporated some Gourock–Kilcreggan passenger-only sailings on a RNAD contract for workers building the new submarine base at Coulport in their routine. From September 1974, *Jupiter* started a run from Gourock to Rothesay two- or three-times weekly, conveying a gas tanker. These went on until *Saturn* had settled on the Wemyss Bay–Rothesay route in May 1978.

In January from 1976 onwards, *Jupiter* undertook a Clyde River Steamer Club charter; on 3 January 1976 to Loch Goil and off Arrochar; 3 January 1977 to Loch Striven and Largs; 2 January 1980 to Tighnabruaich, returning via Garroch Head, a call at Millport (Old Pier) and the Largs Channel; 3 January 1983 to off Ormidale, to mark the 50th anniversary of the club's first cruise and 3 January 1984 to off Garelochhead, Dunoon, Innellan and a cruise to off Ardentinny. In 1976 both were used on occasion of the Ardyne–Wemyss Bay sailings. In 1977 both were on the Wemyss Bay–Rothesay run, replacing *Glen Sannox* on occasion. In 1981 *Juno* was used on the CRSC New Year charter, this time on 2 January to off Lochgoilhead, Rothesay and Kilcreggan, and again on 2 January 1982 to Tarbert with time ashore.

Saturn entered service on 2 February 1978 on the Wemyss Bay–Rothesay service. On 29 April of that year she operated a CRSC charter to Tarbert and Ardrishaig from Gourock, with calls at Rothesay and Tighnabruaich to celebrate the centenary of the paddle steamer *Columba*.

In 1981, the government threatened to withdraw the subsidy for the Gourock–Dunoon service, instead giving a grant to Western Ferries for a new ferry and giving them a subsidy for a fast passenger service from Gourock to Dunoon using the catamaran *Highland Seabird*. There were 376 objections to the proposals, and the STUCC rejected them. In February 1982 it was announced that a subsidy would be paid for an hourly passenger service on the Gourock–Dunoon crossing, and that the company would have to operate the vehicle ferry commercially. The service from then on was hourly, except at the morning and evening peaks; these extra sailings being combined with the Kilcreggan sailings in what became known as the 1A roster. The 1A roster later included a Dunoon–Wemyss Bay crossing and about three Wemyss Bay–Rothesay return trips in the middle of the day, returning to Dunoon for the evening peak. In June 1981, *Jupiter* took over *Glen Sannox*'s inter-resort sailings for the month, with the exception of Brodick, where she did not have a passenger certificate to operate. She called instead at Tighnabruaich. She was laid up for the remainder of the summer. In 1982 she was fitted with a radio-telephone and additional fire-fighting equipment, gained a passenger certificate to serve Arran and was on the Ardrossan–Brodick service after *Clansman* broke down on 28 July. On six

Saturdays in 1983 she acted as a back-up ferry, with an early afternoon Wemyss Bay–Brodick trip, a Brodick–Ardrossan return sailing and returning to Wemyss Bay at the end of the day.

From 1985 *Juno* and *Jupiter* ran a number of charter sailings to the US Navy depot ship in the Holy Loch, carrying heavy equipment including cranes and portakabins. Summer 1985 saw a limited cruise programme by *Jupiter*, sailing from Gourock to Dunoon, Wemyss Bay, and Rothesay, then continuing on Tuesdays to Dunoon with a cruise to Loch Long and on Thursdays to Tighnabruaich with time ashore. By now the three units were all working on both services, e.g., *Juno* was the Rothesay ferry in much of 1986, and *Jupiter* the same in autumn 1988. From 1996 the three vessels changed rosters weekly.

Juno called at Helensburgh on a charter on 23 June 1988 and *Saturn* called from there to Rothesay on 8 June 1996. On 1 June 1990 *Saturn* had a special charter carrying dignitaries from Glasgow (Anderston Quay) to Rothesay for the reopening of the Winter Gardens there. On 25 July 1990, 1 September 1994, 3 September 1995, 6 July 1996, 20 September 2007 and 5 October 2008, she made a series of special short cruises from Gourock to view the Cunard liner *Queen Elizabeth II*, which was lying at Greenock container terminal. On the 1996 occasion she sailed from Gourock to Rothesay to see the liner depart.

On 1 September 1990, she was on a charter from Gourock to Inveraray. On 28 September 1991 *Jupiter* was on a charter to Waverley Excursions Ltd, replacing *Balmoral*, from Gourock, Dunoon and Largs to Rothesay Illuminations. On 8 June 1991, *Saturn* was on a charter from King George V Dock to Rothesay. On 4 April 1992, *Saturn* made a special trip from Wemyss Bay and Largs to Millport for the reopening of the Old Pier.

Following the sale of *Keppel*, cruises were again offered by *Jupiter* from 1993, with sailings on Tuesdays and Thursdays to Tighnabruaich including ninety minutes ashore. On 12 June 1993 the programme *Songs of Praise* was recorded on board *Jupiter*. A Sunday trip to Tarbert was added to the cruise programme in 1994, which was now shared by the three streakers. In 1999, the cruise programme was revamped with Tighnabruaich cruises now on Mondays, Wednesdays and Fridays; a cruise to Millport, or a cruise round Cumbrae if Millport Pier was inaccessible because of low tide on Tuesdays and one to Tighnabruaich and Tarbert, with no call at Largs, on Thursdays. From 30 July until 2 August 1999, *Saturn* made special cruises from Gourock to view the Tall Ships event that was visiting Greenock, and on 2 August a cruise to see them depart. The Millport cruise was not repeated in 2000 and was replaced by a sail round the resorts. The final year in which the cruises operated was 2000, with the last one being to Tarbert on Sunday 24 September by *Saturn*.

Jupiter was laid up at Rosneath on 2 September 2005, following the arrival of the new *Bute* on the Rothesay service. She was reactivated on 2 June 2006, and *Juno* went to Rosneath to be laid up on 11 November 2006. From 19 June to 21 August 2006, *Saturn* served as a second vessel on the Brodick service; she was laid up at Rosneath from 9 December 2006 after she had run a special cruise to see the launch of *Loch Shira* at Fergusons yard at Port Glasgow on the previous day. *Juno* returned to service on 9 January 2007 on the Rothesay service whilst work was done on the berthing facilities there, returning to Rosneath on 21 April. *Saturn* was again on the Brodick service in the summer from 2007 to 2011, and, on 15 September 2007, made berthing trials at Port Ellen, Port Askaig, and Kennacraig. She returned to Rosneath

on 12 November having spent the spring serving Rothesay, and the autumn serving Dunoon. From June 2006 *Jupiter* was full-time on the Dunoon service, apart from overhaul periods, until 12 October 2010 when she was laid up at Rosneath.

Juno was sold to DRB Marine Services Ltd, the owners of the berth at Rosneath, on 21 April 2011 and was scrapped on the beach there. *Jupiter* was sold to Fornæs Shipbreaking of Grenaa, Denmark on 24 June 2011; she was towed there on the following day, arriving there on 1 July and was soon broken up. *Saturn* made her final sailing on Cowal Games day, 27 August 2011, on charter to Argyll Ferries Ltd. from Gourock to Dunoon, where she berthed at the new Argyll linkspan on the breakwater. She then sailed for Rosneath to be laid up and is still there at the time of writing.

Pioneer

Pioneer was built by Robb Caledon at Leith and entered service on 19 August 1974 on the route from West Loch Tarbert to Port Ellen, Islay with calls on certain sailings at Gigha. She was initially a larger version of the streakers, with one crane on each side to handle cargo at Gigha. She had a capacity of 273 passengers and thirty cars. In early February 1975 she relieved *Iona* on the Barra/Boisdale run from Oban. On 25 June 1978, her mainland terminal moved to the Western Ferries terminal at Kennacraig. On her overhaul at her builder's yard in February 1979, her cranes were removed and a hydraulic hoist was fitted aft of the superstructure. The bridge deck was extended aft to the funnels to enable embarkation at low tide. In summer 1979 she moved to the Mallaig–Armadale service, and from the following winter was a general relief vessel in the Clyde and Western Isles, covering most routes there when the regular vessel was off for overhaul. She also made special livestock sailings as required, including some from Canna to Oban, normally twice a year, and from Craighouse, Jura to Oban. She was on the Small Isles service from 5 to 22 May 1980 for the first time, relieving *Lochmor*, although she did not do the Kyle of Lochalsh sailings. On 2 March 1981 she touched rocks at Lochboisdale and lost a rudder. On 14 November 1982 she made a special trip from Gourock to Campbeltown to load heavy equipment. By 1982 her winter duties were confined to the Dunoon and Kilcreggan 1A roster and Islay services, and the annual Small Isles sailings in May (in later years in February), plus occasional Arran and Rothesay sailings when a ferry had broken down or was stormbound. She had special charters in connection with special train trips from England on 15 May 1982 from Kyle of Lochalsh round Skye, calling at Raasay and Armadale, and on 12 May 1984 from Mallaig to Kyle and back. For the first fortnight of October 1984 she ran thrice-weekly from Oban to Colonsay.

14 June 1989 was her final day on the Mallaig to Armadale service; later that month her hoist was removed and side ramps were added. From now on until 1994, she was used as a spare vessel all year round. On 30 January 1990, she gave a charter sailing from Dunoon to the US Navy base in the Holy Loch. In late October and early November 1990, Wemyss Bay Pier was closed for repairs and she joined the three streakers on a Gourock to Rothesay service. On 7 September 1991 she made her first call at Ardrishaig, replacing *Saturn* on an excursion from Gourock. In the first half of February from 1991 to 1993 she was a second vessel on the Arran service, helping *Iona* while *Isle of Arran* was being overhauled. By 1993 she was spending most of her time on the Dunoon and Rothesay services. On 4 June 1993 she sailed from Gourock to Douglas, Isle of Man,

carrying motor cycles for the TT races, thus replacing the Isle of Man Steam Packet's *Lady of Mann* which had broken down. On 20 June 1993 she deputised for *Iona*, making a special sailing from Mallaig to open the re-opened Canna Pier. On 4 September 1993 she made a special cruise from Gourock, Dunoon, Rothesay and Largs to Campbeltown, and on the following day made her first call at Inveraray on a trip from Gourock, Dunoon and Rothesay.

Pioneer became the second Rothesay ferry in 1994, sailing during the summer months; she also did a twice-weekly sailing from Rothesay to Brodick, and a cruise round Holy Isle on Mondays (until 1995) and Thursdays (in 1994 only). She was on the 1A roster in the winter months and continued her annual spell serving the Small Isles. On 13 August 1995 she had a special sailing to celebrate her 21st birthday, sailing from Rothesay, Wemyss Bay and Largs to Campbeltown. On 29 September 1995 she made the final RNAD sailing to Kilcreggan – although CalMac Kilcreggan sailings continued for a further two weeks, the route thenceforth was served by Clyde Marine Motoring with *Kenilworth*. In 1997 the Brodick cruise also operated on Fridays and called at Largs. In 1998 she was on the Mallaig–Armadale service from 30 March, including evening sailings to Castlebay and Lochboisdale from the start of the summer timetable on 10 April. She spent a day on the Uig Triangle on 19 April and eight days from Oban to Craignure and Colonsay from 20 April. She was on the Rothesay route briefly on 27 June for the World Pipe Band Championships, and returned to the Armadale service until 4 July when she returned to Rothesay for the remainder of the summer. On 27 April 2000 she gave a special sailing from Port Askaig to Colonsay, returning to Kennacraig to rescue passengers who had been stranded because of the cancellation of *Isle of Arran*'s call on the previous day due to weather conditions. From April 2001 she was permanently on the 1A roster. On 3–4 October 2002 she stood in on the Armadale service, and again from 4 April to 17 August 2003 until the new *Coruisk* entered service. On 31 August 2003, a special farewell cruise took her from Gourock via Largs Channel, the Tan, between Millport and the Wee Cumbrae, and Garroch Head at the south end of Bute, returning via the Kyles of Bute. She returned to Mallaig to stand in for a sick *Coruisk* on 2 September, remaining there until 18 October when she went to the Small Isles service while *Lochnevis* was overhauled. Her final day in service was there on 1 November, and she retired to the James Watt Dock to be laid up.

She lay there until she was sold to Corlett Line Limited and renamed *Brenda Corlett*. She was to serve the islands of Sao Tome and Principe, off the west coast of Africa in the Gulf of Guinea. She sailed for there on 24 December 2004. She is registered in Senegal. In July 2006 she helped return refugees to Liberia from Ghana. In November 2006 she was to run from Banjul to Dakar and Praia in the Cape Verde Islands, but did not operate this due to engine problems and instead ran from Tiko in Cameroon to Calabar in Nigeria. She has continued on this service ever since, although in early November 2014 she appeared to be under repair near Vlissingen, Holland. On 12 February 2015 she was back in Calabar.

Coruisk, Bute and Argyle

A new, unusual-looking ferry, *Coruisk*, was built by Appledore Shipyards Ltd in Devon in 2003 for the summer service from Mallaig to Armadale, and for winter relief duties on the Dunoon and Rothesay services. She is a cross between a larger version of *Loch Shira* and a smaller version of *Argyle* and *Bute*. Her exhaust uptakes were initially white, but were painted in CalMac colours while she was lying at Gourock prior to her entering service. She entered service on 17 August 2003. On 24 August she lost power and ran onto rocks at Mallaig, where she lost an Azi-pod, and sailed for the Clyde for repairs four days later. It was 11 November before she gave her next passenger sailing on the Dunoon service. She continued operating on the Gourock–Dunoon and Wemyss Bay–Rothesay services in the winter months. Between April and October she operated Mallaig–Armadale route until the advent of the passenger service to Dunoon by Argyll Ferries in 2011; she then served Rothesay only in the winter months. From the 2012/2013 winter she has been chartered to Argyll Ferries to provide peak-hour passenger services between Gourock and Dunoon, also relieving when necessary on the Rothesay service.

Bute, the first of two ferries ordered from the Remontowa shipyard in Gdansk, Poland for the Wemyss Bay–Rothesay route, entered service on 11 July 2005. Her sister *Argyle* started in the route on May 2007. Each can carry 60 cars and 450 passengers; the passenger accommodation is far superior to the streakers, with enclosed passenger lounges fore and aft with a shop and café counter, open-deck space aft on that deck, and an open-upper deck with seating. *Argyle* differs from her sister in having two passenger lifts to the car deck instead of the one on *Bute*, and in the open-deck seating on the accommodation deck facing aft rather than forward as in her sister. They have been thirled to the Wemyss Bay to Rothesay route, apart from occasional weather-related diversions to Gourock. However, repairs to Wemyss Bay Pier for three months from September 2015 will necessitate the service running to Gourock for that period.

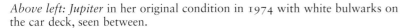

Above left: Jupiter in her original condition in 1974 with white bulwarks on the car deck, seen between.

Above right: Jupiter with the 'GOUROCK DUNOON FERRY' logo, a much criticised logo, on her hull in 1976.

Right: Jupiter off Wemyss Bay in 1984 with nothing painted on her hull.

Above left: Jupiter arrives at Gourock in 1996 with the Kilcreggan ferry *Kenilworth* at the pier.

Above right: Jupiter at Rothesay with the Caledonian MacBrayne logo on her hull, unusually berthed post side in to the pier.

Left: Juno at the inside berth, the old *Kylemore* berth, at Rothesay in the late 1970s on a gas tanker sailing.

Left: Juno departing Rothesay from *Waverley,* 1992.

Above: The launch of *Saturn* from the Ailsa yard at Troon, 30 June 1977.

Above left: Saturn departing Rothesay in 1981 with 'ROTHESAY FERRY' painted in her hull.

Above right: Saturn departing from Rothesay in 1998 with the Caledonian MacBrayne logo on the hull.

Left: Saturn and *Jupiter* laid up at Rosneath in 2007.

Above left: The car deck of *Saturn* as she bids farewell to Dunoon on her final day in service as the Gourock to Dunoon car ferry, 29 June 2011.

Above right: Pioneer in her original condition in West Loch Tarbert. Note the MacBraynes truck on the car deck and the folding ramp.

Right: Pioneer in 1974. Note the crane used to unload cargo at Gigha Pier prior to the service from Tayinloan commencing.

Above left: Sheep coming off a lorry on the car deck of *Pioneer* at West Loch Tarbert, 1974.

Above right: Pioneer departing Kyle of Lochalsh on the Round Skye charter, 15 May 1982 with MacBrayne trucks on the pier and the Kyleakin ferry *Kyleakin* (1970) moored there.

Left: Pioneer at Raasay on the Round Skye charter, 15 May 1982.

Above left: Pioneer at Tobermory.

Above right: Pioneer departing from Mallaig, spring 2003.

Right: Coruisk on the Mallaig–Armadale crossing, 1 May 2004.

Coruisk off Armadale, with *Waverley* berthed there, 1 May 2004.

The Wemyss Bay to Rothesay ferry *Bute*, 2005.

Left: Argyle off the entrance to Loch Striven.

Right: Argyle or *Bute* off the new Rothesay linkspan, showing her hooped black top funnel arrangment.

Chapter 4

LARGE FERRIES

Suilven

Suilven was built in 1974 at the Moss Rosenberg yard at Moss in Norway. She had been ordered as *Bastø VI* by Rederi A/S Alpha of Moss for the crossing across the Oslofjord from Moss to Horten, but the berths were too large for her and she was sold on the stocks to CalMac for the Stornoway–Ullapool service. CalMac had originally been interested in her sister *Bastø V* which was for sale, but modifications to meet UK safety standards were deemed to be too costly so they purchased her unbuilt sister instead. She entered service on 29 August 1974 and offered a twice-daily crossing on the route in summer and once-daily in winter. She was well-suited to the route – although her passenger accommodation was limited to one deck, she had a large vehicle capacity and was well-suited to carry the many commercial vehicles on the route. She could carry 500 passengers and 120 cars. She served the route well and only left it for her annual overhaul. From 9 to 15 October 1989 she was on the Oban–Craignure service, have been replaced on the Stornoway run during the Mod by *Isle of Mull*, which had a higher passenger capacity. On 11 and 12 August 1991 she ran from Uig to Lochmaddy after *Hebridean Isles* had broken down at Tarbert.

She had her last sailing for CalMac on 29 July 1995 and was sold on 22 August of that year to a subsidiary of New Zealand operator Straits Shipping, for a service across the Bass Strait from Wellington to Picton. She entered service there on 16 October 1995. In April 2004 she was sold to Bligh Water Shipping, a Fijian operator, to operate from Suva, Fiji, to Savusavu and Taveuni. In 2012 she was advertised for sale and although it was thought that she would be sold for demolition, she was sold to Venu Shipping to be refurbished and returned to the same service, which she did on 30 August 2013 after eighteen months out of service.

Claymore

Claymore was built by Robb Caledon at Leith and entered service from Oban to Castlebay and Lochboisdale on 3 January 1979. She could carry 500 passengers and fifty cars, and was a larger development of the design of the streakers and *Pioneer*, with a forwards accommodation block, and a hoist and open-car deck with a stern ramp aft of that. The hoist and side ramps were necessary because many of the piers she served did not have linkspans at that time. In the winter she also ran from Oban to Coll and Tiree, and in the summer was on an express run to Lochaline (1979 only), Castlebay and Lochboisdale. On 11 and 13 April 1980, she sailed from Oban to Port Askaig for livestock and repeated that in subsequent years. She occasionally made extra runs from Oban to Craignure or called there to or from the Outer Isles. On 27 April 1986 she sailed from Oban and Lochaline to Tobermory for the Mull Music Festival. Heavy commercial vehicle traffic saw a number of additional overnight runs to Lochboisdale over the years. In her spring 1989 refit, the open deck under the bridge was opened up to passengers and her funnels received silver exhaust pipes.

On 16 June 1989, she started working on the Kennacraig–Islay service. From 20 July to 19 August 1989 she was on the Mallaig–Armadale service in place of the broken-down *Iona*, and from 16 October to 18 December 1989 was on the Oban–Craignure and Oban–Colonsay services, apart from the period from 8 to 23 November when she was on the Uig Triangle. From 10 February to 7 March 1990 she relieved *Isle of Arran* on the Ardrossan to Brodick service, followed by the *Lord of the Isles* on the Barra/Boisdale and Coll and Tiree services from Oban from 12 to 31 March. She replaced *Iona*, which had bow-thrust problems, on the Mallaig–Armadale service from 6 to 30 July 1990 and did a Mallaig–Lochmaddy sailing on 27 July after *Hebridean Isles* had broken down, returning to Uig overnight.

From 26 October to 12 November and again from 2 to 14 December 1991, she was on the Oban to Craignure and Colonsay roster. She was spare vessel from 21 August 1993, when *Isle of Arran* took over the Islay service. From 27 to 29 August 1993 she was on the Wemyss Bay–Rothesay run and made two extra trips from Dunoon to Gourock on the evening of 28 August to clear the Cowal Games traffic. On Saturdays from 28 May to 3 September 1994, and a similar period in 1995 and 1996, she ran a weekly service from Ardrossan to Douglas, Isle of Man, returning on Sunday afternoons. On 19 June 1994 she had an evening charter from Troon to Rothesay Bay and the Kyles of Bute. From 12 to 19 November 1994 she gave a special hoist-loading Wemyss Bay–Rothesay service because of damage to the linkspan at Rothesay.

On the night of 4 September 1995, she sailed to Llandudno and undertook two days of charter sailings for the Hamilton Oil Company to oil rigs in Liverpool Bay. The second day was intended to show a party of American VIPs the lifting of a module onto the upright legs of an oil rig, but bad weather intervened and she undertook a six-hour coastal cruise instead. From 5 to 11 April 1996, she was on the 1A Dunoon roster and also did some Wemyss Bay–Rothesay sailings after *Juno* had trouble with one of her Voith-Schneider units, and again on 22 and 23 April after *Juno* had broken down. On 7 May 1996 she took a party of American rhododendron enthusiasts from Dunoon to Brodick and Tarbert; she repeated this on 9 May, this time completing her charter at Ardrishaig, her intended final call on the previous occasion which had been unavailable then because of low tide. On 2 June 1996, she was on charter to the Isle of Man Steam Packet Company to convey motor cycles from Heysham to Douglas for the TT races, and again on 9 June to return them to the mainland. From 2 to 6 July 1996 she was chartered to run between Dun Laoghaire and the US navy aircraft carrier *John F Kennedy*.

On 22 April 1997, she made her final sailing for CalMac from Kennacraig to Port Ellen. On 1 May she was sold to the Argyll and Antrim Steam Packet Company, a subsidiary of Sea Containers Ltd., for a new twice-daily service from Campbeltown to Ballycastle. One of the conditions of the sale was that she be returned to CalMac under charter each winter, and she came back to the Islay service from 30 October to 19 December 1997. She was on her new service from 30 June to 18 October 1997, from 8 May to 1 June and from 12 June to 11 October 1998, being on charter to Honda UK for a Heysham–Douglas service during the TT races from 2 to 11 June, with evening cruises from Douglas from 8 to 11 June. She was on the Ballycastle service again from 14 June to 18 September 1999. The service ceased after that season and she was laid up at Birkenhead in February 2000. From 16 May 2000, she was on a five-week charter in the Faeroes.

In August 2002 she was sold to Pentland Ferries and operated a passenger and freight service from St Margaret's Hope to Invergordon from 11 to 29 November 2002. She was then laid up, being reactivated for the Gills Bay service from 7 March to 3 April 2003 and from 1 November 2003 to 3 June 2004, initially on a twelve-passenger basis, but with a winter certificate for 71 and summer for 250 from 19 January 2004. She was on the route again from 10 November 2004 to April 2005 and for a similar period in subsequent winters. From June to October 2006 she was on charter to Farmers Ferry Ltd for livestock sailings from Dover to Boulogne and Dunkirk. In 2007 she remained on the Pentland Firth service until 21 November. In her overhaul that month she lost her hoist and side ramps and her hull was painted red. She was back in service again from 11 January 2008 to 29 March 2009, with spells off for overhaul in December and from 29 January to 12 February 2009.

At the end of March 2009 she was sold to the Danish company CT Offshore, renamed *Sia* and converted to be used as a cable layer. The addition of four bow-thrusters made her extremely manoeuvrable in her new role. She is now used for laying cables for wind farms in the North Sea.

Isle of Arran

Isle of Arran was built by Ferguson-Ailsa Ltd at Port Glasgow for the Ardrossan–Brodick service and could carry 228 passengers and seventy-six cars with bow and stern ramps. She had been launched in an unusual grey livery, but this was painted the usual black at a dry-docking whilst being fitted out. She entered service on 13 April 1984 and remained on the Arran service, with occasional stormy weather diversions to Gourock, until 25 August 1993. In her initial season and until her dry-docking in April 1985, her black hull-paint continued up to promenade deck level. From 1 to 27 October 1984 and 1 to 20 October 1986 she relieved *Suilven* on the Ullapool to Stornoway service.

On 1 February 1993 she undertook berthing trials at Kennacraig, Port Ellen and Port Askaig, and took over the Islay service on 26 August 1993 and replaced the broken down *LOTI* on the Castlebay–Lochboisdale and Coll–Tiree sailings from 30 August until 25 September 1993. She replaced *Hebridean Isles* for overhaul on the Uig Triangle from 8 to 26 November 1993 and on a similar period in subsequent years until 1997. On 23 July 1994, she took an evening charter from Port Ellen round the Mull of Oa to off Port Charlotte. From 27 September to 18 October 1994 she relieved *Caledonian Isles* on the Arran service for overhaul. In March 1998 her black hull-paint was stepped so that it was a deck higher from below the bridge to the bow. From 21 to 24 July 1998, most of her sailings ran to and from Oban instead of Kennacraig, because the A83 was closed north of Tarbert due to repairs following a landslide, and the diversion via Kilberry was unsuitable for heavy vehicles. On 17 December 2000 she struck an unidentified floating object in deep water four miles west of Gigha and damaged her starboard propeller. There was no relief ferry available, and *LOTI* had to make special sailings from Oban to Port Askaig until she returned from repair on 21 December. She underwent berthing trials at Stornoway on 12 March, 2001 en route for overhaul at Aberdeen and at Ullapool on the return journey. She was then relieved on the Uig services and following *Hebrides*' entry into service, she became spare vessel and was laid up in James Watt Dock, Greenock. On 22 September 2001 she undertook an army charter from Ardrossan to Campbeltown, returning on 29 September.

She was the second vessel on the Stornoway service from 11 November 2001 to 8 April 2002, allowing *Isle of Lewis* to be in service less than twenty-four hours a day. From 23 June to 28 August 2002 she was based at Oban as a third vessel, running to Castlebay and Lochboisdale, to Port Askaig via Colonsay and to Castlebay via Tiree, as well as extra sailings on the Craignure service. From 19 July she offered two cruises weekly from Oban, a castles cruise on a Friday, round Lismore and Kerrera with a call at Craignure, and a cruise to the Gulf of Corrievreckan and Colonsay on a Monday. From 29 August 2002 she was back on the Islay service returning to the Stornoway cargo service from 1 November 2003 to the end of the month, and was then laid up at Stornoway until 4 February 2004. She continued as second Islay ferry during the summer and spare vessel throughout the network in the winter months and from October 2007 was secondary Islay ferry all year round.

From 27 October until 29 December 2011, following the entry into service of *Finlaggan*, she started a spell on the Stornoway freight service again. She was then laid up at Campbeltown when not in use as a spare vessel throughout the network. From 19 to 23 January 2012 she was on the Arran service, helping out *LOTI* during a period of poor weather, and called uniquely at Wemyss Bay on 22 January. She was there again from 12 to 22 February after *Caledonian Isles* had been damaged whilst berthing at Ardrossan. From 2012 she has been the second vessel in the summer months on the Arran service, in that year serving in a freight-only role from Monday to Friday and only carrying passengers on Saturdays. From 21 to 23 September 2012, the Glasgow holiday weekend, she was on the Wemyss Bay–Rothesay service. On 23 May 2013 she inaugurated a new summer service from Ardrossan to Campbeltown, sailing from Ardrossan on Thursdays and Friday evenings and returning the following morning, with a return sailing on Sunday afternoons. The Saturday sailing from Campbeltown also calls at Brodick. From 26 January to 5 February 2014, she was on the way to Greenock for her annual overhaul and was called in to relieve on the Arran service after *Caledonian Isles* had broken down. From 22 February to 7 May 2014 she was on the Stornoway service after *Isle of Lewis* had damaged her port rudder and had had to sail for Birkenhead for repairs.

Hebridean Isles

Hebridean Isles was built by Cochrane Shipbuilders Ltd of Selby and was launched sideways by the Princess Royal on 4 July 1985, being the first vessel in the fleet to be launched by royalty, and the first to be launched sideways. She has bow and stern loading and a hoist aft of the funnels, with side-loading ramps and has space for 507 passengers and sixty-eight cars. She entered service on 5 December 1985 on the Stornoway–Ullapool route, relieving *Suilven* which was away for overhaul and remained there until 12 January 1986. She then did berthing trials at Port Askaig, Port Ellen, Kennacraig and Colonsay before taking up the Oban to Craignure and Colonsay service on 29 January, where she remained until early May. On 3 May, she gave a special sailing for journalists and a Clyde River Steamer Club party from Oban round Mull, calling at Tobermory. On 9 May she moved to her intended route, the Uig Triangle and remained there until 2000, relieving *Suilven* on the Stornoway route from 12 to 31 October 1987, and at a similar time of year in 1988. On 27 July 1989 she gave the first of what would become an annual event, a charity evening cruise from Tarbert to the Shiant Islands. In 1993 this sailed to off the Skye coast. On 11 April 1992 she was chartered to run from Lochmaddy to Stornoway, carrying 400 protesters who were complaining about the removal of the only surgeon from Dalhousie Hospital in South Uist. From April 1996, sailings on the Tarbert to Lochmaddy leg of the route ceased after the

Sound of Harris ferry service came into operation. From 1 to 25 March 2000 she relieved on the Islay service.

On 8 March 2001 she gave her last sailing on the Uig routes and moved to become the Islay ferry, a service on which she continues. On 31 August 2002 she was on the Wemyss Bay–Rothesay service. From 30 September 2002 until 21 April 2003, she was on charter to Northlink for the Scrabster to Stromness service, as the new *Hamnavoe* was delayed at her builders' yard. She then returned to the Islay service, sharing it with *Isle of Arran* from 23 May 2003. From 7 to 26 February 2004, and similar periods until 2007, she was on charter to Northlink to relieve *Hamnavoe* on the Pentland Firth crossing. From 17 June to 30 July 2010 she operated out of Oban, after *Clansman* had broken down, on an amended roster to make up for her lack of speed compared to her newer fleet-mate.

Isle of Mull

Isle of Mull was built by Ferguson's at Port Glasgow and had space for 1000 passengers and eighty cars. Whilst fitting out, it was discovered that she was 114 tonnes deadweight overweight. She was sent to the Tees Dockyard at Middlesbrough on 2 October 1988, where she was lengthened by 17.1 feet and could then hold a further seven cars, returning to service on 6 December. She had entered service on the route from Oban to Craignure on 11 April 1988, along with Colonsay sailings, and has continued on that service to the present day. She has occasionally served Castlebay and Lochboisdale when *Lord of the Isles* was under repair, or when the traffic was too much for her. From 9 October to 7 November 1989 she was on the Stornoway run during the Mod Gaelic music and poetry festival to give additional passenger capacity. On a similar spell from 1990 to 1994 she was on the Stornoway–Ullapool service and relieved *Suilven* for overhaul and *Isle of Lewis* similarly in 1996 and 1997. From 28 October to 11 November 1991, she sailed from Stornoway to Uig because of problems with the Ullapool linkspan. In the early hours of 22 August 1992, and on the subsequent night, she visited the new Tiree linkspan to pick up lambs for market, a task which would become an annual routine for her. On 3 July 1993 she was on an evening charter from Oban to Loch Linnhe and on 2 July 1994 to Loch Buie. On 28 August 1993 she substituted for *LOTI*, which had broken down, and made her first call at Coll. On 14 October 1996 she had an evening charter from Oban for the Highland Cattle Society. From 19 April to 14 May 1998 she was on the Ullapool–Stornoway service after *Isle of Lewis* had had a major breakdown. From 29 November to 19 December 2007, she relieved *Caledonian Isles* on the Arran service.

Lord of the Isles

Lord of the Isles (LOTI) was built in 1989, again by Ferguson's at Port Glasgow, and entered service on 22 May from Oban to Castlebay and Lochboisdale and Oban to Coll and Tiree, on three days per week each in the winter with more sailings to Barra and South Uist in the summer timetable. She can carry 506 passengers and fifty-seven cars and has bow and stern ramps and a hoist aft of the superstructure. Occasionally she has swapped rosters with *Isle of Mull* and operated to Craignure and Colonsay. New linkspans were opened at Coll on 5 June 1992 and Tiree on 29 June 1992. From 1 to 4 December 1997 she was on the Uig service replacing *Hebridean Isles* which was undergoing bow thruster repairs at Stornoway. Calls at Tobermory ceased on 9 April 1998.

Replaced by the new *Clansman*, she moved to the summer Mallaig–Armadale service on 6 July 1998, including a twice weekly overnight sailing to Castlebay and Lochboisdale, returning to the Oban to Barra/Boisdale and Coll and Tiree runs in the winter months. From 1999 the summer Outer Isles sailings were given on a Sunday evening to Barra and on a Tuesday evening to South

Uist. From 17 to 21 December 2000, she ran from Oban to Port Askaig, combining this with the Craignure and Colonsay rosters. From 29 October to 11 November 2001 she was the second ship on the Stornoway service. From summer 2002 the Armadale roster did not include Outer Isles sailings and on 1 November 2002 she made her final Mallaig–Armadale crossing.

From summer 2003, she was based at Oban as the second Coll–Tireee–Colonsay vessel also operating the castles cruise during the summer timetable period and stayed at Oban year-round, while *Clansman* was touring the network as relief vessel during the winter months. In 2004 the Gulf of Corrievreckan cruises were discontinued and two castle cruises were given each week, a long one for bus parties on a Tuesday and a short one to Craignure via the south of Kerrera and back direct on a Wednesday. She and *Clansman* had a more equally shared roster from that summer. From 29 April to 3 May 2004 she was on the Rothesay service for the Bute Jazz Festival. In summer 2006, she offered an Oban–Tobermory cruise on most Tuesdays with time ashore. She relieved *Hebridean Isles* on the Islay service from 13 November to 2 December 2011, and 10 November 2012, and was on the Arran service from 5 to 19 January 2012. From 10 November 2013, twice-weekly return crossings on Tuesdays and Saturdays from Lochboisdale to Mallaig and back were added to her winter schedule, although inclement weather has meant that many of these sailings have been cancelled.

Caledonian Isles and Isle of Lewis
Caledonian Isles was the new Arran ferry built by Richards of Lowestoft. She is considerably larger than *Isle of Arran* and can carry 1,000 passengers and 1742 cars. She entered service on 17 August 1993 and has served the Ardrossan–Brodick route faithfully ever since. On 6 January 1996 she made a charter cruise from Brodick to the Cock of Arran for the Clyde River Steamer Club, repeating this on 4 January 1997 with a cruise off to Whiting Bay and round Holy Isle. On 21 January 1997 she performed a Burns Supper evening cruise from Brodick to Ardrossan via the Largs Channel.

A new, larger, Stornoway ferry, *Isle of Lewis*, built by Ferguson Brothers of Port Glasgow, entered service on 27 July 1995. She can carry 968 passengers and 123 cars. She made 18.92 knots on trials and can make three return crossings daily from Ullapool to her namesake island when required with a scheduled passage time of 2 hours 45 minutes. On 18 April 1998, when she was on charter to carry army vehicles for an exercise on North Uist, her port engine seized whilst at Lochmaddy; she had to sail for the Clyde for repairs on one engine and did not return to service until 14 May. In November 1998 she was at A. & P. Tyne Ltd. at North Shields for overhaul, calling at Aberdeen on the way there and Stromness on the homeward journey. From 26 January to 17 February 2009 she was overhauled at a yard at Fredericia, Denmark. On 19 July 2009 she made the first scheduled Sunday service to Stornoway, provoking anger from some religious hardliners in the island.

Clansman and Hebrides
Clansman, a new ferry for the Outer Isles service from Oban, was built by Appledore Shipbuilders Ltd. in Devon and entered service on 4 July 1998 on the Oban to Coll and Tiree service. She also sailed to Castlebay and Lochboisdale. During the 1998/1999 winter she was the fleet reserve vessel. On 9 January 1999, whilst relieving on the Arran service, she was on a charter to the Clyde River Steamer Club from Brodick to off Pladda and round Holy Isle, with similar charters on 15 January 2000 round Cumbrae; 5 January 2000 and 12 January 2001 to Lochranza Bay; 12 January 2002 round Inchmarnock and to off the Cock of Arran, and 11 January 2003 round Arran. She was on the

Uig services from 8 to 24 March 2001 after *Hebridean Isles* had left for the Islay run and prior to *Hebrides* entering service.

From 11 to 27 November 2002, she was on the Stornoway service while *Isle of Lewis* was overhauled. In the summer of 2003 she exclusively served Castlebay and Lochboisdale in the summer timetable period, with only two Coll and Tiree sailings per week. She also undertook the Gulf of Corrievreckan and Colonsay cruises that summer. Since 2004 the sailings from Oban, apart from Craignure, have been shared more equally between her and *LOTI*. On 17 June 2010, she suffered serious damage to the crankshaft of one engine, and had to be withdrawn for repairs, not re-entering service until 30 July.

Hebrides, a quasi-sister of *Clansman*, was built at Ferguson's at Port Glasgow, was launched by Her Majesty the Queen on 2 August 2000, entering service from Uig to Tarbert and Lochmaddy on 24 March 2001. She can carry 600 passengers and 118 cars. From 10 to 14 November 2003 she ran from Lochmaddy to Ullapool while the Uig linkspan was under repair (Tarbert passengers and vehicles were diverted via Stornoway). In March 2007 her engines were converted to burn a heavier grade of fuel oil, and she ran from Oban to Castlebay and Lochboisdale and Coll and Tiree from 2 to 7 April to run the new system in. From 23 October 2011 a Sunday service was recommenced from Tarbert to Lochmaddy, on what had previously been a positioning run, thus restoring the old triangle service. During the 2012/2013 winter she was the relief vessel and made her first call at Colonsay on 3 December 2012 whilst relieving *Isle of Mull* in January 2015, which she relieved on the Ardrossan to Brodick service.

Hascosay, Muirneag and Clipper Ranger

In 2001, there was competition on the Ullapool to Stornoway service from a company called Taygran Shipping which operated the chartered cargo roro *White Sea* (1972) from the early part of the year, replacing her with *Taygran Trader*, formerly *European Trader* (1975) of P&O European Ferries. The rivals took a large part of the traffic from *Isle of Lewis*, and it must have come as a relief to CalMac when they closed down on 7 August of that year when the ship was arrested.

CalMac then decided to place a dedicated freight vessel on the Ullapool–Stornoway route and firstly chartered the 1971-built *Hascosay* from Northlink. She was sent to the Remontowa yard at Gdansk for a major overhaul and entered service on 8 May 2002 with a night-time crossing in each direction. Her final crossing was on 27 September 2002, as Northlink's franchise started on 1 October and she was required for their services.

She was replaced by the chartered *Muirneag*, a 1979-built cargo roro vessel, owned at that time by Harrisons (2002) Ltd. and formerly operating for P&O from 1985 to 1993 from Belfast to Ardrossan under the appropriate name *Belard*, which entered service on 28 September 2002. She was painted with a blue hull and the CalMac lions on her funnels were initially painted the wrong way round. She made her final sailing for the company on 20 September 2013 and was replaced by *Clipper Ranger* (1998), chartered from Seatruck Ferries, which continues on the route.

Finlaggan

A new ferry for the Islay service, *Finlaggan*, was built in 2011 at the Remontowa shipyard at Gdansk in Poland. She has clamshell bow doors, a first in the CalMac fleet, and can carry 550 passengers and eighty-five cars. She entered service on 1 June 2011 from Kennacraig to Port Askaig, but suffered from hydraulic problems after less than a fortnight, having to go to Cammell Laird at Birkenhead for repairs. From 22 to 25 April 2012 she visited many of the ports in the CalMac network for berthing trials, sailing as far north as Stornoway and Ullapool. Her final call was at Castlebay, an intended call at Lochboisdale was cancelled because of the weather, and she gave an emergency service from Castlebay to Oban on 26 April because *Clansman* was stormbound at Oban. From 1 December 2012 to 31 March 2013 and again from 3 to 24 January 2015, she was relief vessel on the Uig services.

Loch Seaforth

A new ferry for the Stornoway service named *Loch Seaforth* was built in 2014 by Flensburger Schiffbau-Gesellschaft MBH at Flensburg in Germany. She was delivered in November 2014 after running a series of trials in the North Sea and the Irish Sea, but was laid up at the Inchgreen wharf at Greenock, unable to enter service because the berthing facilities at Ullapool and Stornoway had to be altered for her. She can carry 700 passengers and 143 cars and is 10 per cent faster than Isle of Lewis.

She entered service on the overnight freight sailing on 10 February 2015, her first passenger sailing being on 13 February. The Stornoway car-ferry service is due to be diverted to Uig from 22 February to 7 April 2015, and Loch Seaforth is scheduled to provide a passenger-only service from Ullapool in that period, while *Isle of Lewis* and *Clipper Ranger* will be sailing to and from Uig.

In October 2014 it was announced that the Scottish Government had authorised CalMac to order two new large ferries, each to carry 1,000 passengers and 127 cars, for the Uig and Arran routes respectively. At the time of writing no orders had been placed for these. Planned delivery is December 2017 and mid-2018 respectively.

Claymore on the stocks at the Rob Caledon yard at Leith in 1978 with Mrs Margaret Langmuir, wife of the noted author Graham E. Langmuir.

Above left: Claymore at the fitting out berth at Robb Caledon, 3 December 1978.

Above right: Claymore departing Port Askaig for Oban 24 June 1993, with *Pioneer* in the background.

Left: Claymore at Victoria Pier on one of her visits to Douglas, Isle of Man, for the TT races.

Above left: Claymore in Argyll & Antrim Steam Packet Co. colours at Rothesay with the company crest below the bridge.

Above right: Claymore at St Margaret's Hope with *Pentalina B* (ex *Iona*) leaving.

Right: Stornoway ferry *Suilven* in Loch Broom.

Left: Isle of Arran, still in her grey undercoat, fitting out at Greenock with a yellow disc and a lion outline on the funnel.

Above: Isle of Arran at Brodick in her original colour scheme in 1984.

Above left: Isle of Arran, the pot at the end of the rainbow, at Brodick in 1990.

Above right: Isle of Arran in her current condition, spring 2004.

Right: Isle of Arran at Kennacraig with *Saturn* on berthing trials, 16 September 2007.

Above left: Hebridean Isles arriving at Oban as *Eigg,* with heightened wheelhouse, departs for Lismore.

Above right: Hebridean Isles at Wemyss Bay, 31 August 2002.

Left: Hebridean Isles departs from Stromness with *Hamnavoe* at the pier.

Isle of Mull passing the Hutcheson Monument on Kerrera.

Isle of Mull departing Oban, spring 2002.

Above left: Lord of the Isles at Wemyss Bay, 2004.

Above right: Lord of the Isles off the Knoydart coast, 2004.

Left: Lord of the Isles in Rothesay Bay, 1 May 1999.

Above left: Lord of the Isles amongst moored yachts, off Armadale, 1 May 1999.

Above right: Caledonian Isles at speed, 2001.

Right: Caledonian Isles departs Brodick, 12 August 2010.

Above left: Caledonian Isles at Brodick, spring 2006, prior to the most recent extension to the pier.

Above right: Caledonian Isles in the James Watt Dock, Greenock, 1993.

Left: Isle of Lewis on the stocks at Ferguson's, Port Glasgow, a few days before her launching on 18 April 1995.

Above left: Isle of Lewis at Ullapool, September 1995.

Above right: Clansman at Brodick with a snow-covered Goat Fell, 9 January 1999.

Right: Clansman at Brodick, 11 January 2003.

Above left: Clansman off Kerrera as she departs from Oban, 10 June 2009.

Above right: The launch of *Hebrides* at Port Glasgow, 24 March 2001.

Left: Hebrides fitting out at Port Glasgow, spring 2001.

Above left: Hebrides off Tarbert, Harris 24 June 2011.

Above right: Muirneag biting into a storm in the Minch.

Right: Muirneag arriving at Stornoway.

Above left: Finlaggan at Kennacraig, 14 July 2011.

Above right: Finlaggan at Port Askaig with the Argyll and Bute Council ferry *Eilean Dhuira*, which runs to Feolin on Jura, 6 August 2011.

Left: Loch Seaforth newly arrived from her builders, off Greenock (Custom House Quay) 7 November 2014. (Gordon Law)

Chapter 5

SMALLER FERRIES
The Island Class Bow-Loading Ferries

The eight Island-class ferries, known by some as the 'daft ducks' were all built between 1972 and 1976 by James Lamont & Co. at Port Glasgow. The first two, *Kilbrannan* and *Morvern*, were 63-feet long, with a capacity of five cars and fifty passengers. The remainder were 68-feet long with a capacity of seven cars and seventy-five passengers. A small passenger cabin was provided aft. They were used to open up new routes to the islands which, in most cases, have had to be taken over by larger ferries of the Loch class as traffic developed. They were difficult to load as cars had to be reversed to get on to them, this being a problem at places with steep slipways and at low tide. From the autumn 1999 overhauls the black paint on the hull of the remaining four vessels was raised to the lower edge of the car deck.

Kilbrannan
Kilbrannan, the first of the eight, had entered service on 8 July 1972 on the newly introduced summer-only route from Lochranza to Claonaig on the Kintyre peninsula. New slipways had been

built at both ends of the route over the previous four months. She relieved on the Largs–Cumbrae Slip and Port Askaig–Feolin, Jura routes doing the winter months. On 28 June 1973, she was replaced by *Rhum* at Lochranza and moved to the Largs–Cumbrae Slip service as a spare vessel, where she also substituted for *Keppel* on occasion on the passenger service to Millport (Old Pier). She was on the Scalpay service from 2 June 1977 until 8 June 1990, regularly overhauling at Stornoway. After she left the Scalpay service, she was spare vessel on the Clyde, spending most of her time laid up at Shandon. On 24 June 1990 she conveyed a tractor from Campbeltown to Sanda. From 16 June to 16 August 1991, she relieved on the Burtonport–Aranmore service in County Donegal in the Republic of Ireland. On 20 August 1991 she conveyed a bulldozer to the island of Wee Cumbrae from Largs.

On 5 June 1992 she was sold to Cornelius Bonnar of Aranmore, County Donegal, to serve on the Burtonport–Aranmore service and renamed *Arrain Mhor*. She was sold in 2008 to Clare Island Ferries and renamed *Clew Bay Queen*, operating from Roonagh Quay, south-west of Westport to Clare Island and to Inishturk, mainly on crane-loaded cargo sailings, although also used on passenger sailings to Clare Island in the peak summer season.

Morvern

Morvern entered service on 2 April 1973 on the Largs–Cumbrae Slip service and moved to the new Fishnish–Lochaline service on 1 May, but was replaced by the larger *Bruernish* on 19 May. She was on the Oban–Lismore service from 14 October, replacing *Loch Toscaig*, whose engine had been removed. In the first half or 1977 she was on an emergency Tarbert–Scalpay service while the slipway at Kyles Scalpay was being rebuilt, and served there until 3 June, having operated on the normal route from 11 April. From 17 November 1977 until 25 April 1979 she was on the Lismore service and operated the car-ferry service from Fionnphort to Iona from 22 May 1979. She did this until the introduction of *Loch Buie* on 9 June 1992, while also tendering to *Columba* and cruise ships as required. Her car deck was laid out with wooden seats for this duty, and she was certificated for 142 passengers. On 9 November 1990, she carried sixteen Highland cattle and what should have been seventeen Eriskay ponies from Holy Isle to Brodick, although twelve of the ponies escaped and had to be left on the island. From June 1992 she was a spare ferry, laid up at Shandon when not in use to relieve other vessels. In spring 1993 she relieved the two Western Isles Council car-ferries *Eilean Bherneraigh* and *Eilean na H-Oige* and the latter again in spring 1994.

From 16 to 20 June 1995 she was chartered for the Ballycastle–Rathlin service in connection with a wedding on the island, and on 24 July she was chartered to Cornelius Bonnar for the Burtonport–Aranmore route. He purchased her six weeks later and she was sold in 2001 to Bere Island Ferries, to run from Castletownbere to Bere Island. She later returned to the Aranmore service, where she now operates for Aranmore Fast Ferry.

Bruernish

Bruernish entered service on 19 May 1973 on the Lochaline–Fishnish route, remaining there until she was replaced by *Coll* on 19 December when she then relieved *Lochnell* on the Tobermory–Mingary service. She carried large lorries from Oban to Craignure during the period from October to December 1974, when *Columba* was on the Craignure route. She was then on various routes and from 28 November to 12 December 1976 was on a new passenger-only service from Kyle of Lochalsh to the Howard Doris oil platform yard in Loch Carron, serving on the Kyle–Toscaig service in the afternoons. From 9 January to 6 May 1978, she ran from Kyle to the accommodation ship *Rangatira*, with portakabins on the car deck and also maintained the Kyle–Toscaig service. On 17 and 18 May 1978 she made a total of three runs from Mallaig to Inverie on Loch Nevis with heavy equipment.

On 2 February 1979 she commenced a temporary service from Kennacraig to Gigha South Pier, and started operating from Tayinloan to the new slipway at Ardminish on 14 November 1980, serving that route until 13 September 1992. On 26 October 1992 she picked up the ponies left on Holy Isle almost two years before by *Morvern*. Afterwards *Bruernish* had a spell acting as relief vessel moored at Tobermory when not in use elsewhere, giving extra sailings to Kilchoan in the summer of 1993 and 1994. On 24 July 1994 she took construction plant and a tractor from Tobermory to Calve Island and on 12 and 18 August 1994, she took contractor's material out to and back from Rhu na Gal lighthouse. From 23 September to 8 October 1994 she relieved *Eilean na H-Oige*, which had broken down, on the Ludag–Eriskay service. On 29 May 1995 she made an experimental crossing from

Ludag in South Uist to Ardveenish in north Barra, during a period when she was relieving the two Western Isles Council ferries.

On 1 July 1995 she made a crossing from Crinan to Ardlussa in Jura, with eighty-eight soldiers en route to an overnight exercise there. From 1 December 1996 she started a ferry service on charter to the Northern Ireland Office from Ballycastle to Rathlin, operating there until 22 April 1997 when she moved to the Portavadie service for the summer. From 16 January to 12 October 1998 she was on the Lismore service and was a relief vessel from 1999 onwards. On 14 May 2000 she carried some vehicles from Colintraive to Inchmarnock. From 2001, she spent much of her time laid up at Shandon and only saw nine days service in 2003. Her final day in service was 10 March 2003, relieving *Eigg* on the Lismore service.

On 25 September 2006, she was sold to Humphrey O'Leary for service at Clare Island. She has had a period on charter to Aranmore Fast Ferries, and currently she reportedly serves a fish farm on Clare Island.

Rhum

Rhum entered service on 28 June 1973 from Lochranza to Claonaig. From 5 November to 15 December 1973 she operated a service from Portree to Raasay, replacing the Portree leg of *Loch Arkaig*'s itinerary. She relieved on various services over the next couple of years and was on the Lismore service in the first few months of 1976, and on Lochranza–Claonaig in the summer timetable period from 1977 to 1986. She regularly relieved on the Fishnish–Lochaline services in the spring, and was on the Kennacraig–Gigha service in autumn 1979 and Tayinloan–Gigha in autumn 1981. On 15 May 1982 she was chartered by the Clyde River Steamer Club for a trip from Lochranza to Carradale, which was the first call there

by a passenger vessel since 1939. From 1987 she was relief vessel for the Western Isles, and remained moored in the bay at Tobermory when not in use.

On 15 September 1988, she made several trips from Girvan to Ailsa Craig and again on 24 and 25 August 1989 to Ailsa Craig from Largs. From the summer of 1990 until the arrival of *Loch Buie* in June 1992, she was second vessel on the Iona service in the summer months and was then a relief ferry. From 30 June until 22 July 1992 she tendered to *Waverley* at Brodick while work was being done on the pier. From 25 March to 7 May 1994 she was on charter to the contractors building the Skye Bridge, transporting cement from the contractor's slips at Plock of Kyle and Kyleakin Quarry to the bridge site. From 23 to 25 March she had been the only operational ferry on the Kyle–Kyleakin service. She started a summer Tarbert–Portavadie service across Loch Fyne on 7 July 1994, and on 16 October 1995 she started a new winter service from Tarbert to Portavadie, with one return crossing to Lochranza and three returns from Lochranza to Claonaig on Tuesdays. She was replaced on this on 3 November by *Loch Striven*. From 5 April to 29 October 1996 she was on the Tarbert–Portavadie service. She moved to the Scalpay service on 17 March 1997 but was withdrawn from that when the service ceased after a new bridge was opened to the island on 16 December 1997.

Her last sailing for CalMac was on 15 January 1998 from Oban to Lismore and back, and she was sold on 17 April of that year to Cornelius Bonnar for the Burtonport–Aranmore service, which she still serves for Aranmore Ferries.

Coll

Coll entered service on 15 November 1973 from Oban to Craignure, replacing the broken-down *Columba*, until the arrival of *Bute* on the evening of the following day. She then relieved

Loch Arkaig on the Small Isles service until 16 December. She then moved to the Lochaline–Fishnish service, as she had radar (unlike *Bruernish*, which did not have radar fitted until her 1974 overhaul). She also made special sailings to Oban in the middle of the day with heavy vehicles, but from April 1974 these were replaced by an extension of one sailing a day from Fishnish to Craignure. She was then a general relief ferry in the Western Isles and returned to the Small Isles service from 17 March to 12 May 1979. She closed the Kennacraig–Gigha service on 7 November 1980 and opened the new service from Tayinloan to the slipway at Ardminish on Gigha on 10 November. From the summer of 1985 she was on the Tobermory–Mingary service, carrying passengers only, with fifty-six rigid plastic seats being temporarily affixed to the car deck. In 1987 and 1988 she offered cruises from Mingary to Ardnamurchan on Tuesdays, and Loch Sunart on Thursdays and Sundays (the latter in 1987 only).

From 1989, Mingary was referred to as Kilchoan in the CalMac timetable. On 29 April 1991 she inaugurated a new car ferry service from Tobermory to Kilchoan, concrete ramps having been built at both ends of the route. From 5 to 10 March 1992 she operated an experimental service in Northern Ireland from Ballycastle to Rathlin. From October 1994 the Tobermory–Kilchoan service became the year-round home of *Coll*, although in the 1995/1996 winter it only ran three days a week. From 16 January 1996 to 16 December 1997, she was on the Lismore service.

She was sold on 2 February 1998 to Cornelius Bonnar for the Burtonport–Aranmore service, which she still serves for Aranmore Ferries.

Eigg

Eigg entered service on 25 February 1975 as a spare vessel on the Kyle–Kyleakin service. She was on the Lismore route from 19 March 1976 to 6 January 1996. On 14 June and 19 July 1981 she conveyed construction gear and a digger to and from Inverliever on Loch Etive. She also operated occasional runs to Craignure, e.g. to convey a fire-engine at 12:30 a.m. on 17 April 1981. She also operated a regular petrol-tanker run to Craignure, occasional livestock runs from Lochaline to Oban and trips to the quarry at Glen Sanda. She also made an annual trip, from 1984, with sheep from Eigg, and on some occasions from Muck, to Glenuig, near the mouth of Lochailort. She made regular trips to a fish farm on Kerrera as well and went to Easdale with road material on 5 March 1989.

From January 1996 she was a reserve ferry, berthed at Tobermory. She was then on the Kilchoan summer service from 1996 to 1998. From the 1996/1997 winter, the Kilchoan service did not operate in the winter timetable period. From 19 November to 18 December 1998 she operated from Mallaig to Eigg and Muck, while the Eigg flitboat *Ulva* was away for overhaul. She returned to the Lismore service on 21 December 1998. In spring 1999, her wheelhouse was raised a deck above the previous position so that the helmsman could see above the top of the lorries with loads of hay that frequently used the service. Her black paint was raised to the bow during August 1999, but reverted to the earlier scheme at her 2000 refit. In early 2001 she was re-engined at Shandon, and she remained on the Lismore service until December 2013 when she was replaced by *Loch Riddon*. From October 2008 a Sunday service was operated, which put a stop to the Craignure fuel-tanker runs. She made an annual visit in the spring until 2009 to the Port Askaig–Feolin service, when she was chartered to Argyll and Bute council to relieve *Eilean Dhuira* for overhaul. She is currently spare ferry at Oban, available to relieve *Loch Striven* at low tide when she cannot access the slipway at Lismore.

Canna

Canna entered service on 2 February 1976 on the Portree–Raasay route and inaugurated the new service from Sconser to

Raasay on 16 April 1976. She moved to the Fishnish service on 7 October of that year where she stayed until 4 July 1986, when she was replaced by *Loch Linnhe*. From 7 to 22 April 1987 she was chartered to the Orkney Isles Shipping Co. to run trials on the Kirkwall–Shapinsay service, and again from 28 March to 3 May 1988. On the 20 April to 31 May 1977 she was chartered to relieve *Eynhallow* on the Rousay, Wyre and Egilsay service. She was spare vessel on the Cumbrae service in the summer of 1987 and was then laid up at Shandon. From summer 1988 she was a second ferry on the Iona service, berthing overnight at Bunessan. From 18 April to 3 June 1990 she was on both Orkney services. From 8 June 1990 she moved to the Scalpay service, where she was until 15 March 1997.

She took on the Ballycastle–Rathlin service on 22 April 1997 and continues there to this day. She was re-engined at the Timbacraft yard at Shandon in November 2000. In 2008, with the reorganisation of Caledonian MacBrayne, a new company named Rathlin Ferries was set up to operate the service. She has operated from 1 July 2008 on charter to Rathlin Island Ferries, a new company set up by Ciaran O'Driscoll, who is the operator of the passenger ferry to the island.

Raasay

Raasay, the final member of the Island class, entered service on 30 May 1976 as a stand-by vessel on the Cumbrae Slip service on 30 April 1976. She took over the Sconser–Raasay service on 9 July 1976, and served there until 4 May 1997, when she was replaced by *Loch Striven* and became a spare ferry for the summer. She returned to Raasay on 15 September of that year for the winter. In November and December 1999 she operated from Mallaig to Eigg and Muck and was an Oban-based spare

vessel from 2000 onwards. She was fitted with new engines in the summer of 2003. From 29 October 2003 she has been on the winter Tobermory–Kilchoan service and has also relieved *Lochnevis* on the Mallaig to Small Isles route. The Island class operated many one-off sailings to unusual locations in the West Highlands and islands both with cargo and for use in repairing berthing facilities, and also operated on services other than their own from time to time, particularly on their way to the Clyde for overhaul, or on the way back. They were small enough to pass through the Crinan Canal.

Eilean Bherneraigh and Eilean na H'Oige

Eilean Bherneraigh had been built in 1983 for Western Isles Council to operate the service from Otternish to Berneray. In 1996 the route was taken over by CalMac; she was chartered by them but retained her blue hull, with a Caledonian MacBrayne banner hung across the side of the car deck. On 17 December 1998 a new causeway from North Uist to Berneray opened and her service ceased. She moved to be a spare vessel on the Ludag–Eriskay run until the causeway was opened in 2003 to replace the ferry service. She was sold in August 2003 to the Transalpine Redemptorists to assist in the rebuilding of the monastery at Papa Stronsay on Orkney. They renamed her *Sancta Maria*. She was later sold to Bere Island Ferries, and remains in operation from Castletownbere to Bere Island under the name *Sancta Maria*.

Her sister *Eilean na H-Oige* relieved her for overhaul from 9 to 13 March 1998. She had been built in 1980 for the Ludag–Eriskay service and was sold in August 2003 to Bere Island Ferries in the Republic of Ireland, to run from Castletownbere to Bere Island. She now appears to be the reserve ferry there, and has been renamed *Oilean na h-Oige*.

Above left: Kilbrannan lying inside Largs pier, with *Waverley* at the pier face, 1973, and *Queen Mary II* approaching in the background.

Above right: Morvern tendering towards *Waverley* off Iona, 7 May 1990. *Morven, Kilbrannan, Coil, Bruernish,* and *Rhum* have all tendered to *Waverley* in the Sound of Iona, also *Rhum* at Brodick in 1993 whilst the pier was being built (see p.83). *Loch Buie* tendered at Iona in 1994 but proved unsuccessful.

Left: Clew Bay Queen (ex *Kilbrannan*) loading cargo at Roonagh for Clare Island, 23 July 2013.

Above: Morvern at Burtonport, 24 July 2013.

Right: Coll at the Oban slipway, 1997 with *Lord of the Isles* at the linkspan.

Above left: Rhum at Tarbert, Loch Fyne in spring 1995.

Above right: Rhum at Burtonport, 24 July 2013.

Left: Bruernish departing from Largs in summer 1975.

Above left: Bruernish at Tobermory with *Coll* moored in the bay, 1994.

Above right: Bruernish in black-hulled condition, departing from Kilchoan.

Right: Eigg, with heightened wheelhouse along the side of Oban North Pier, unusually at the top and beached, 2002.

Eigg leaving Oban on 9 September 2007, showing to good advantage her heightened bridge and funnel.

Canna along the side of Largs pier, 1999.

Left: Raasay inside Largs pier, 1989.

Right: Raasay in black-hulled condition off Iona, heading for Fionnphort.

Chapter 6

SMALLER FERRIES
Double-Ended Ferries: The Loch Class

Isle of Cumbrae
CalMac's first double-ended ferry, *Isle of Cumbrae*, which counts as an honorary Loch-class ferry, entered service on 7 April 1977 from Largs to Cumbrae Slip. She had been built by Ailsa Shipbuilding Co. at Troon, and had capacity for 160 passengers and eighteen cars. She initially had an all-white livery, and in her February 1987 refit her wheelhouse was painted red and black like the four 1986 Lochs. She provided much needed extra capacity on the Cumbrae service. On 1 and 14 April 1983 she visited Millport (Old Pier) with Calor Gas canisters, occasionally sheltering there and at Keppel Pier in stormy weather.

She remained at Largs apart from overhaul and repair periods until 3 August 1986 when she moved to the Lochaline–Fishnish service. She returned to the Cumbrae slip service on 4 November 1986. She was on the Fishnish run again from 7 May 1987 and moved to Kyle of Lochalsh on 25 November 1987 as a relief ferry and continued on this pattern until 1995. From 5 to 17 August 1989, she was on the Kyle crossing after *Lochalsh* had had a major breakdown. From the 1995/1996 winter onwards she was on the Fishnish service year-round. From 19 July 1997 she moved to the Colintraive–Rhubodach route and from 11 to 24 September 1997 she was back on the Cumbrae Slip service. She then returned to the Rhubodach service and on 27 November was back at Lochaline. In 1998, she was on the Cumbrae Slip service from 20 March until 11 May, and the Colintraive–Rhubodach crossing from 13 May 1998 until 25 January 1999, moving on 31 March 1999 to the summer Portavadie service which she maintained until replaced by *Lochinvar* in 2014. On 20 October 2003 she started a new winter service from Tobermory to Kilchoan, but was only on it for ten days before moving to the Rhubodach service for the whole of November. She relieved *Loch Dunvegan* at Colintraive until 2005, and *Loch Fyne* at Lochaline until 2007. From the arrival of *Lochinvar* on 7 May 2014 until November 2014, she was kept on standby at Tarbert in case of the former vessel breaking down.

Loch Striven
In 1986 four double-ended ferries were delivered by Richard Dunston Ltd. of Hessle on the river Humber. They could carry twelve cars and 203 passengers each.

The first to enter service was *Loch Striven*, which started on 4 July 1986 as a second ferry on the Cumbrae Slip service, and took over the Colintraive–Rhubodach crossing on 31 October 1986 for just over a week. She then moved to become spare ferry at Kyle of Lochalsh until January 1987, when she relieved *Loch Riddon* for overhaul then went back to the Cumbrae service full time. On 21 September 1987, she made a special cruise to Wee Cumbrae to celebrate the opening of the new pier buildings at Largs. From the 1995/1996 winter onwards she was on the new Tarbert–Portavadie and Tarber–Lochranza–Kilchoan roster, started by *Rhum* (q.v.), returning to the Cumbrae Slip service in the summer period. From 28 July until 14 September 1997, she was on the Sconser–Raasay service, then relieved on various services over the winter and was back serving Raasay from 9 April 1998 until replaced by *Hallaig* in November 2013. On 10 June 2014, she moved to the Oban–Lismore service full-time.

Loch Linnhe

Loch Linnhe entered service from Fishnish to Lochaline on 4 July 1986, moved to the Cumbrae Slip service on 4 August and returned to the Lochaline route on 5 November. From 15 May to 28 October 1987 she was the second ferry on the Cumbrae Slip service, then she returned to the Fishnish service for the winter. On 30 March she returned to Largs and stayed there through the remainder of 1989, apart from a spell relieving on the Colintraive service. From then on she tended to relieve the other three Lochs for refit and spent the remainder of the year mainly on the Cumbrae service, but was on Fishnish–Lochaline in the winter months when *Isle of Cumbrae* was at Kyle until late 1995. She was then on overhaul relief sailings in the winter months, often lying at Tobermory between these. She was on the Portavadie service from 27 March to 24 October 1998, and then relieved *Loch Buie* on the Iona service to 19 November. From 30 April 1999 she has been on the Tobermory–Kilchoan service in the summer months and has been the winter-relief vessel. She inaugurated the new service from Eriskay to Ardmhor, Barra, on 4 April 2003 and was there until 6 June. She has relieved on that route in February and early March each year from 2010 to 2013. From 29 December 2013 to 6 March 2014 she was on the Tayinloan–Gigha service.

Loch Riddon

Loch Riddon entered service on 28 September 1986 on the Fishnish–Lochaline route, and moved to the Colintraive–Rhubodach route on 7 November 1987. On 16 October 1991, she had to berth at Ormidale during a storm and had to use Rothesay on other occasions. From 26 July 1997 she moved to the Cumbrae Slip service for the summer, and then went to the Lochranza–Claonaig crossing on 10 September for just over a month. She was replaced by *Loch Aliann* at Rhubodach on 26 February 1998, then moved to the Cumbrae Slip service and then to Lochranza from 9 to 21 September, back to Largs, and, after a couple of days back on the Rhubodach service. She was on the Tarbert to Portavadie and Lochranza service from 19 November and continued the pattern of Cumbrae in the summer and Tarbert in the winter until the following year. She continued in this pattern apart from 2000, when she was on the Tobermory–Kilchoan service in the summer and was spare ferry, based at Tobermory in the winter months until November when she went on the Tarbert to Portavadie and Lochranza roster, continuing on this until spring 2001. Her roster includes the regular replacement of *Loch Buie* on the Fionnphort–Iona service in the early or late months of the year.

Loch Ranza

The fourth ferry, *Loch Ranza*, entered service on 16 April 1987 from Lochranza to Claonaig, and operated there until the service ceased on 28 September. She then relieved *Loch Riddon* for overhaul on the Colintraive service until 29 October, and *Loch Striven* at Largs for a few days. In late February and early March each year she was on the Cumbrae Slip service, relieving *Loch Striven* for overhaul. She was a regular fixture on the Lochranza–Claonaig service each summer until the arrival of *Loch Tarbert* in 1992. On 26 September 1992, she took over the Tayinloan–Gigha service from *Rhum* and has remained there until the present day. It is thought she may be replaced by the third hybrid ferry, recently ordered from Ferguson's.

Loch Dunvegan and Loch Fyne

In 1991 two new ferries for the Kyle–Kyleakin crossing were built by Ferguson's at Port Glasgow. Both had a capacity of 250 passengers and thirty-nine cars, *Loch Dunvegan* entered service on 13 May and *Loch Fyne* on 2 August. On 16 October 1995 the Skye Bridge opened and the last ferry crossing was made. The two ferries then went for an extensive period of lay-up at the James Watt Dock, Greenock, and both were put on the sale list. Both were on the verge of being sold to Sierra Leone owners in early 1997, but a coup there put an end to that and it was decided to return them to service.

Loch Dunvegan started operating on the Lochaline–Fishnish service on 19 August 1997. *Loch Fyne* replaced her on that route on 27 September after the former vessel had suffered a serious breakdown and has been there ever since.

1998 was a busy year for *Loch Dunvegan*. She returned to the Fishnish service from 28 January to 14 March, operated a passenger-only peak hour service from Wemyss Bay to Rothesay from 12 to 30 April 1998 and was on the Mallaig–Armadale service from 2 to 14 May and 26 June to 7 July (she also operated this route from 27 August to 2 September 2003 and 8–11 September 2004). Further, she operated the Tarbert–Portavadie run from 20 to 31 July 1998 during a spell when the A83 was closed due to a landslide five miles north of Tarbert. She returned to the latter route from 16 to 23 August, and from 23 October to 1 November. In 1999 she was on the Portavadie service from 24 February to 1 March while the landslip damage was repaired on the A83, and moved to the Colintraive–Rhubodach service permanently on 31 March after a concrete mooring-dolphin had been put in place at Colintraive.

On 15–16 April 2000 *Loch Fyne* conveyed a crane from Tobermory to Corran, and on 13 February 2001 made a call at Lismore to load a high-sided vehicle and take it to Oban. She was at Lismore again on 24 December 2001 with four articulated trucks, each carrying a generator, after the island's power supply failed. *Loch Dunvegan* relieved on the Fishnish service from 11 to 18 February 2012, on her first spell of duty in the West Highlands since 1995. *Loch Fyne* was on the Cumbrae Slip service on 8–10 February 2013.

Loch Buie

A dedicated ferry for the Fionnphort to Iona service was built in 1992 by James Miller of St Monans and named *Loch Buie*. She only has a single lane for cars (visitors' cars are not allowed on the island), has passenger saloons on each side of the hull and a saloon bridging the car deck. She has a capacity of 252 passengers and ten cars, the high number of passengers being useful on the occasions when she connects with the tour bus from Oban. She entered service on 8 June 1992. On 7 November 2000, she gave three emergency services from Lochranza to Claonaig and one to Tarbert, then operated on the Portavadie service until 10 November because *Loch Tarbert* had suffered damage and *Caledonian Isles* was stormbound in Ardrossan.

Loch Tarbert

Another ferry from James Miller of St Monans, *Loch Tarbert*, entered service on 25 July 1992 on the summer Lochranza–Claonaig service. She has three lanes for vehicles rather than the two of the 1986 Lochs, giving her a capacity of twenty-eight cars rather than twelve, along with 150 passengers. She has remained on the route ever since from Easter to late-October and has operated overhaul reliefs in the winter months. On 29 October 1993 she ran trials on the new route from Leverburgh, Harris, to Otternish, North Uist. She then spent a spell relieving *Loch Buie*, and then *Isle of Cumbrae*, which had gone to Kyle as *Loch Dunvegan* had broken down. From autumn 1994 to 2003 she was on the Cumbrae service in the winter months and on 21 October and from 19 to 21 December 1994 provided a sailing from Largs to Brodick with an oil tanker on board, as the MSA had prohibited *Caledonian Isles* from carrying such vehicles.

From 10 September to 2 October 1997, she replaced the broken-down *Loch Bhrusda* on the Sound of Harris service and was there again from 6 March to 4 April 1998 while the regular vessel was away for overhaul. After the 1998/1999 winter she was on the new Tarbert–Portavadie–Lochranza roster, which now included a daily Tarbert–Lochranza sailing

and no calls at Claonaig, although from 2002–2004 and 2007 she only operated this until December each year. On 7 November 2000, she damaged her Voith-Schneider unit on rocks at Tarbert and had to be towed to Greenock for repairs, returning three days later. From 9 to 22 February 2007, and for a similar period in 2008, she relieved *Loch Bhrusda* on the Sound of Barra service.

Loch Bhrusda

A further ferry, *Loch Bhrusda*, was built in 1996 by McTay Marine at Bromborough, near Birkenhead, for the Sound of Harris service from Leverburgh to Otternish. The shallow nature of the waters on the route resulted in her having two Schottel pump jets instead of propellers. She can carry 150 passengers and eighteen cars, and has the wheelhouse above the car deck. She entered service on 8 June 1996. From September 1996 all sailings were extended from Otternish to Berneray, and from the end of September sailings during the hours of darkness were banned by the MSA. From 14 October 1996 to 9 March 1997 she only offered one daily sailing from Leverburgh, running to and from Berneray for the remainder of the day as *Eilean Bherneraigh* was laid up for the winter. In 1997 the top of her bridge was painted bright orange for safety reasons and in summer 1997 almost all Berneray sailings were taken by the chartered *Eilean Bherneraigh*, but *Loch Bhrusda* berthed there overnight, giving the first sailing in the morning to Otternish and the last evening sailing back from there.

On 8 September 1997 she was withdrawn with a major gearbox failure, and it was 2 October before she could re-enter service following repairs. From the 1998/1999 winter and the completion of the causeway there, the Berneray crossings ceased to be made. On 11 April 1999, she made a trial crossing from Ardveenish to Barra to two different points on Eriskay, berthing at Castlebay before and after. From early May 2001 the crossing was from Leverburgh to a new slipway which had been built at Berneray; from 31 August she berthed overnight at the Otternish end of the Berneray causeway rather than Berneray harbour. On 20 February 2003 she berthed overnight at the new mooring at Ardmhor, Barra en route south to her annual overhaul at Troon and started serving on the new route from Eriskay to Ardmhor on 7 June 2003. In late February 2003, the orange paint on the top of her wheelhouse was painted white whilst under overhaul at Troon.

On 4 July 2007 she was replaced by *Loch Aliann* and then became spare ferry, relieving when necessary throughout the CalMac network and laid up at Rosneath when not in service. She was back on the Sound of Barra service from 29 October 2007 to 13 February 2008 and in subsequent winters. On 16 September 2008 she undertook berthing trials at the new slipways at Eigg and Muck, calling at Inverie on 1 October. From 11 to 28 October she was on the Small Isles service, assisted by the chartered *Ullin of Staffa* until 2009, in 2010 by *Sula Beag* chartered from Sealife surveys of Tobermory and since 2011 by *Orion* of Sea.fari of Armadale. She has done this annually since, also in July 2010. On 28 May 2010 she was the first CalMac vessel to call at the new slipway at Raasay, while on charter to Balfour Beatty, to convey heavy equipment involved in its construction from Kyle of Lochalsh. From 13 May to 3 July 2013, she was chartered to Foster Yeoman to make sailings from Barcaldine to Glensanda Quarry.

Loch Aliann

A further new ferry *Loch Aliann*, originally to have been named *Loch Aline*, was built by Buckie Shipyard in 1997. She has conventional Voith-Schneider units rather than the water jets of *Loch Bhrusda*, and can carry 150 passengers and twenty-four cars. She can be distinguished by having a very wide section of her bridge support painted in the CalMac funnel colours. She has a wheelhouse over the car deck and was intended for the Lochaline–Fishnish service, but she entered service on 8 July 1997 on the Colintraive–Rhubodach service as part of a cascade of vessels, following a breakdown by *Canna* on the Rathlin service. She eventually took over the Fishnish service on 19 July. She herself had a major breakdown on 17 August and headed for the Clyde on one engine for repairs. In 1998 she was on the Rhubodach crossing from 25 February and the Cumbrae Slip service from 14 May, where she remained until 2007 (apart from a spell on the Portavadie service from 24 February to 1 March 1999, when the A83 was closed again for repairs). From 26 November to 2 November 2000, and on 25 June 2001, she was on the Gourock–Dunoon 1A roster, on the latter date for passengers only. On 4 July 2007 she took over the Eriskay–Ardmhor service until 29 October. Following that she relieved *Loch Dunvegan* on the Rhubodach service from 6 to 18 November, *Loch Shira* at Largs from 8 January to 1 February 2008 and *Loch Fyne* at Lochaline from 5 February to 5 March, before returning to the Sound of Barra with similar relieving duties in the subsequent winters. She has been on the Sound of Barra service year-round from 22 November 2012.

Loch Portain

A new ferry for the Sound of Harris route, *Loch Portain*, entered service on 5 June 2003. She was built by McTay Marine at Bromborough with her hull having been built in Poland. Like *Loch Bhrusda*, she is propelled by water jets, although she has four rather than the two of her predecessor and so is more manoeuvrable. She can carry 195 passengers and thirty-three cars and has a passenger lounge above her car deck, surmounted by the bridge and wheelhouse. On 7 March 2011 she made a trial return-crossing from Largs to Cumbrae Slip whilst on her way back from overhaul.

Loch Shira

Loch Shira, a new ferry for the Largs to Cumbrae Slip service, was built by Ferguson's at Port Glasgow and entered service on 2 June 2007. She can carry 250 passengers and thirty-six cars, and has a large comfortable passenger lounge above the car deck with a small amount of outside seating fore and aft of this. Initially, prior to Largs Pier being rebuilt, she berthed overnight at Fairlie, or Gourock in adverse weather conditions.

Hallaig and Lochinvar

Two new hybrid ferries with a unique propulsion system, combined a small diesel-engine and rechargeable Lithium-Ion batteries, were built by Ferguson's in Port Glasgow. They can carry 150 passengers and twenty-three cars. The first was named Hallaig and entered service, after an unconscionably long time fitting out, from Sconser to Raasay on 25 November 2013. On 4 April 2014 she operated from Mallaig to Armadale when Coruisk was out of service. The second ferry, Lochinvar, entered service on 27 May 2014 from Tarbert to Portavadie. On 26 July she led the Commonwealth Games flotilla of yachts and motor-cruisers up the Clyde to Glasgow (Pacific Quay). From 26 January 2015 she was on the Largs to Cumbrae Slip service for a couple of weeks or so. A third hybrid ferry was ordered on 26 September 2014 from Ferguson's for delivery in autumn 2016, possibly to go on the Gigha service.

Space does not permit details of the ferries' annual overhauls, most of which have been at the Ardmaleish yard on Bute, with some at Troon (Ailsa in the early years, and now Garvel Troon) and Corpach. Neither is there space for details of the long journeys of several days from the West Highlands to the Clyde with calls including Tobermory, Craighouse, Jura, Kennacraig, Campbeltown and Largs.

Isle of Cumbrae departs Tarbert in late summer 2000.

Left: Loch Striven arriving at Largs, 1984.

Right: Isle of Cumbrae at Tobermory, about to load a fuel tanker.

Above left: Loch Linnhe from *Waverley* off the Ross of Mull on 1 May 2006.

Above right: Loch Linnhe arriving at Tobermory from Kilchoan.

Right: Loch Riddon at Largs slipway, 2002.

Above left: Loch Riddon at Tarbert, Loch Fyne, 1997.

Above right: Loch Ranza at Gigha, 31 May 2011.

Left: Loch Dunvegan resting at Kyle of Lochalsh railway pier, 1995.

Above left: Loch Dunvegan at Rhubodach, 2003.

Right: Loch Fyne at Kylerhea slipway 1995.

Loch Fyne passing the Hutcheson Memorial on Kerrera, inward bound to Oban.

Loch Buie heading for Fionnphort with Iona village in the background.

A broken-down *Loch Tarbert* at Lochranza, with *Loch Riddon* just arrived from Claonaig, 31 May 2011.

Loch Tarbert arriving at Lochranza on 12 June 2010.

Left: Loch Bhrusda at Largs, September 2008, seen from *Waverley*.

Right: Loch Aliann off Largs, 1999.

Above left: Loch Portain off Kerrera, departing from Oban on trials and heading for Lochaline.

Above right: Loch Shira arriving at Largs, with *Waverley* at the pier, 7 August 2013.

Left: Loch Shira at Cumbrae Slip, 30 April 2010.

Left: Hallaig fitting out at Port Glasgow, 26 August 2013.

Right: Hallaig running trials on the Skelmorlie measured mile, 7 August 2013.

Above left: Lochinvar fitting out at Port Glasgow, 16 August 2013, in her original paint scheme.

Above right: Lochinvar on the Commonwealth Games Flotilla passing Braehead Shopping Centre, 26 July 2014.

Left: Lochinvar on a trial service form Tarbert to Portavadie on 23 July 2014.

Chapter 7

OTHER SMALLER VESSELS

On 1 October 1972, David MacBrayne Ltd took over the Fionnphort–Iona passenger ferry service from Alasdair Gibson and three motor launches were purchased in 1973 for this route and also to relieve at Eigg.

Tiger, Craignure and Applecross

Tiger had been built in 1904 as *Elizabeth of Buckhaven* and was purchased from Roy Ritchie of Gourock, for whom she bore the name *Shona*. She was found unfit for further service in early 1975 and sold then. Her engine was believed to have been a test-engine built for John Browns for the lifeboats of No. 534, later the Cunarder *Queen Mary*.

Craignure had previously been owned by David MacBrayne Ltd. from 1950 until the opening of the pier at Craignure in 1964. She had been built in 1943 as *Silver Spray*, for use as a ferry-cum-flitboat at Craignure, and was sold in 1964 to Bruce Watt of Mallaig and then to Murdo McSween of Fort William. CalMac kept her until August 1979 when she was sold to Gordon Grant of Iona for transport of livestock to and from the Treshnish Isles.

Applecross was another former David MacBrayne vessel; she had been owned by them from 1963, when she was purchased for the Kyle of Lochalsh to Toscaig and Kyle of Lochalsh to Kylerhea services. She remained there until 1969 when she was sold to Alasdair Gibson for the Fionnphort–Iona service, having been on the Iona service from 1965. She had been built in 1944 for Bruce Watt of Mallaig as *Highlander*, and was then owned by a man from Glenelg. She originally had a passenger cabin, but this was removed when she was purchased by CalMac and a wheelhouse was fitted above the engine. After the car-ferry service started to Iona in June 1979 she was kept at Iona as a second vessel on the ferry service and to tender to Western Ferries' catamaran *Highland Seabird*. She was moved to Tobermory on 26 May 1981, took over the summer-only Mingary service and tendered the Coll and Tiree ferry at Tobermory. After the closure of the pier on 30 May 1983, she also tendered to *Columba* and to any other vessel calling there. From the reopening of the pier in March 1985, she was purely on the Mingary service until sold on 25 October 1985, back to Alasdair Gibson, now based at Loch Buie, for private use.

Kildonan and Staffa

In 1975, a further two open launches were purchased: *Silver Darling* from Murdo McSween of Fort William, which was renamed *Kildonan* and put into service at Eigg, and *Silver Spray* from Dick's of Largs, which was renamed *Staffa* and based at Iona. Her hull was painted brown rather than the usual red until 1978. *Kildonan* had been built in 1923 as a demonstration launch named *Falcon* for the Bergius Company. In 1979 she was transferred to Lochaline, where she was used on occasion to tender the spare ferry anchored there in Moidar Bay, but was mainly in lay-up state. On 4 and 5 June 1981 she was used to give a passenger-only service from Lochaline to Fishnish when *Canna* was off service, and then returned to lay-up. She was sold in 1985, her engine was removed and she was taken to Ardmaleish.

Staffa was the tender at Tobermory from 7 March to 2 August 1981, and was on the Mingary service from 11 to 25 May 1981. She then had a spell relieving at Eigg and was taken to Shandon and scrapped at the end of August 1981.

In 1988 a similar motor-boat, *Dart Princess*, was purchased from owners at Paignton in Devon for use as a spare flit-boat at Eigg, to relieve *Ulva* for overhaul. She had a wheelhouse forward and was open aft of that. She entered service on 7 September 1988 but broke down after only two days service and was taken to Arisaig for repairs. She also relieved the Nature Conservancy ferry *Rhouma* at Rum, and the island-owned *Wave* at Muck, but spent much of her CalMac career laid up at Shandon or in Tobermory Bay. On 14 October 1992, she broke down in Easdale Sound on her way south after her service at Eigg and had to be towed back to Oban by the Oban lifeboat. He last passenger sailing was on 11 November 1994, tendering to *Lochmor* at Rum, and she was then laid up at Mallaig and put up for sale. She moved back to Shandon on 2 April 1995 and was sold to a private owner in September 1996.

As a new flit-boat and tender for Eigg to replace *Ulva*, *Laig Bay* was built by the Corpach Boatbuilding Co. and entered service on 22 December 2000. She could carry twenty-eight passengers and was much more modern looking than the old Red Boats, having a black hull that was metal rather than wooden. She was moved to Tobermory on 13 May 2004, and tendered to the Kilchoan ferry at night, when the latter lay at a buoy in the bay. She was laid up at Corpach throughout 2005 and was sold in December of that year to Aska Marine of Kyle, which traded as Sea Discoverer, and operated trips out of Kyle of Lochalsh. She is currently up for sale again.

Lochmor

In 1979, a new vessel named *Lochmor* was built to replace *Loch Arkaig* on the Small Isles and Armadale winter service. Built by Ailsa at Troon, she could carry 130 passengers. She had an open deck aft with a crane for cargo handling, and all her passenger accommodation was forward of the funnel. She entered service on 18 July. Initially she also gave a service from Mallaig to Kyle of Lochalsh, with weekly cruises to Loch Duich and to Portree in the summer months. The winter Kyle service was withdrawn on 31 October 1980 and replaced by two more return services to Armadale on most days. From the summer of 1981, a weekly Crowlin Islands cruise was added from Kyle. Frequently sailings to the Small Isles were cancelled or altered because of the weather, especially in the winter months. The Portree cruise was not given from 1985. On 13 April 1987, she was on the Oban–Lismore service in an emergency whilst heading to Greenock for a short lay-up period. The Armadale calls ceased during the summer timetable period when a car ferry was on the Mallaig–Armadale service. The summer timetable was revised from 1994, giving time ashore at some of the islands, and the Kyle sailing was only made on Fridays and the afternoon cruises from Kyle ceased being offered.

On 2 October 1994, she was on charter to the Salmon Growers Association from Kyle to fish farms at Loch Kishorn, the Sound of Scalpay and Loch Ainort on Skye, where she berthed alongside the cages so her thirty-eight passengers could have a better view. On 20 March 1995 she made her first call at Tarbert, Harris to collect a gangway for *Mallaig* and a fender for *Canna*. The Kyle of Lochalsh sailing was not offered after the 1997 season, which is of note because steamers had sailed through Kyle Rhea since the 1820s. On 22 March 1999, she was on charter to Strathclyde Passenger Transport Executive and made berthing trials at Kilcreggan and Helensburgh. She made her final scheduled sailing for CalMac on 18 November 2000 and made a special cargo run to Eigg on 5 December, following which she was withdrawn from service and laid up in Tobermory Bay.

On 15 March 2001 she was sold to a Campbeltown owner, moved to Campbeltown on 16 March and renamed *Lochawe* for a proposed Campbeltown–Ballycastle service. In early July, she was reportedly resold to a Mr R. Beatty of Galway for a proposed service to the Aran Islands and sailed there in the middle of that month, but his plans did not work out and she was sold again in 2002 to Brixham Belle Cruises of Paignton, renamed *Torbay Belle* and was rebuilt with an enlarged wheelhouse, new saloon and bar on the main deck, a new upper deck with a bar and an extended funnel. She operated from 2004 to 2008 on cruises form Torquay and Brixham to Dartmouth. In 2009 she was sold to Blue Line Cruises of Poole and renamed *Jurassic Scene*, and operated trips from Poole and Bournemouth to Swanage, with occasional trips to Yarmouth, Isle of Wight, and visited Southampton on charter. In 2014 she was sold to the Icelandic company Sea Ranger, and renamed *Gullfoss* to operate whale-watching trips form Akranes and Reykjavik, being laid up at Reykjavik in the winter months.

Lochnevis

A new stern-loading ferry for the Small Isles, *Lochnevis*, was built by Ailsa Troon Ltd in 2000. Slipways were to be provided at Eigg, Muck and Rum for her. She can carry 200 passengers and fourteen cars. Her passenger accommodation is far superior to that on *Lochmor*, with a very spacious passenger lounge and cafeteria. She is rather ungainly looking with a very tall stern-ramp. She entered service on 20 November 2000. Due to her increased speed compared to her predecessor, her timetable was recast and day trips with time ashore were now possible to all four islands. She also gave a limited car-ferry service to Armadale in winter. It was originally intended that she also serve Inverie in Loch Nevis, but that did not materialise. It was not until 2004 that the new slipways were completed, making the flitboats and tenders redundant. She ran berthing trials at Inverie on 18 November 2007. On 10 May 2009 she undertook a special sailing to Lochboisdale for the Ministry of Defence, and on 28 June 2009 she was chartered for a special sailing from Castlebay along the coast of the Western Isles as far as Mingulay. On 24 and 25 July 2010 she again crossed to Castlebay for the Barra Festival, as *Clansman* was out of service for repairs, calling at Canna en route on the latter date. She repeated this on 28 July and on 1 August, calling at Canna in both directions. It was not until the 2010–2011 timetable period that she was first scheduled for Sunday sailings, and that just a single afternoon return sailing to Armadale; it was summer 2013 before there was a Sunday service to the Small Isles.

Ali Cat

The passenger catamaran *Ali Cat* was chartered in October 2002 from Red Funnel Ferries, who had in turn chartered her from Solent and Wightline Cruises (Blue Funnel) of Ryde, Isle of Wight. She was built in 2000 by South Boats of East Cowes, Isle of Wight and can carry 250 passengers at a speed of 16 knots. She was placed on the Gourock to Dunoon 1A roster, now a passenger-only one, with two morning returns and one evening peak hour crossings. She lay in the James Watt Dock at Greenock when not in use. Passengers were embarked at the Kilcreggan ferry berth at Gourock and the linkspan at Dunoon pier. On 14 June 2003, she was chartered to Clyde Marine for a cruise from Greenock (Victoria Harbour) and Helensburgh to an open-day at the Faslane submarine base. She was chartered by them again on 6 July 2004 to take a coach party from Sandbank to Tighnabruaich and back.

On the third Saturday of August each year from 2004 to 2010, she gave additional sailings from Wemyss Bay to Rothesay for the Bute Games weekend. On the last Saturday of August from 2003 to 2005, and from 2007 to 2010, she gave additional sailings on her route for the Cowal Games. On 4 September 2004 she was chartered to the Clyde River Steamer Club for an afternoon cruise from Gourock, with calls at Sandbank, Kilcreggan, Wemyss Bay, Millport, Largs and Helensburgh. On 15 and 16 July 2006 she ran from Braehead to Glasgow Science Centre as part of the Festival of the Sea. She has regularly visited the Kip Marina at Inverkip for repair and maintenance. On 20 September 2008 she was chartered to the Clyde River Steamer Club for an afternoon cruise from Gourock to Blairmore, the Gareloch and Kilcreggan, and

again on 19 September 2009 from Gourock to Tighnabruaich, Loch Striven and Rothesay.

In January 2010, she was on charter to the BBC for a trip to the laid up container ships in Loch Striven in connection with a children's programme. On 24 June 2011, she was purchased by David MacBrayne Ltd. and operated from 30 June for Argyll Ferries on the new passenger-only half-hourly Gourock to Dunoon service, along with *Argyll Flyer*. This called at the new Argyll linkspan on the southern breakwater rather than the steamer pier.

Argyll Flyer

Argyll Flyer was purchased on 13 June 2011 from Aran Island Ferries Ltd. She had been built as *Queen of Aran II* in 2001 at the OCEA yard at Les Sables d'Olonne in western France, and later renamed *Banrion Chonamara* (Queen of Connemara). She is a fast aluminium-hulled monohull and can carry up to 244 passengers and has a speed of 19.7 knots, although she is restricted to 12 knots north of the Cloch. She entered service on 14 July 2011 and has maintained the Argyll Ferries Gourock–Dunoon service ever since with occasional disruptions for weather and continual murmurings from the people of Dunoon who are demanding the return of a vehicle ferry.

Chartered Vessels

Clyde: There has been a steady flow of vessels on short-term charter on the shorter Clyde routes over the years. These have included:

Countess of Kempock	14 April 1973	Gourock–Kilcreggan
Kenilworth	6 July 1998	21:15 Wemyss Bay–Rothesay and possibly on other occassions
Rover	5 May–2 July 1998	17:45 Gourock–Dunoon and return
Rover	16 September 1998	Largs–Millport (Old) after *Loch Aliann* had broken down
The Second Snark	5 May–2 July 1998	17:45 Gourock–Dunoon and return (shared with *Rover*)
The Second Snark	13 and 20 June and 4 July 1998	21:15 Wemyss Bay–Rothesay
Rover	11 September 1999	12:00 and 13:35 Largs–Millport (Keppel)
The Second Snark	13 January 2000	16:15 and 18:00 Largs–Millport (Old)
Clyde Clipper	28 June–5 July 2011	Gourock–Dunoon (Argyll Ferries) Also 25 August 2012 31 August 2013 and 30 August 2014 (Cowal Games Saturday)

West Highlands: again the charters have been, in the main, on the shorter routes:

Puffer *Marsa*	1974 (several times)	Oban–Gigha with cargo until *Pioneer* entered service
Glenmallie (Glenelg ferry)	1973–1976	Relieved Scalpay for overhaul for two weeks each October
St Oran (J & A Gardner)	21–27 April 1998	Oban–Craignure with cargo
St Oran (J & A Gardner)	29 June 1998	Castlebay–Mallaig with fish lorries
Wave (Muck tender)	13–21 Sept 1999	Tendered at Eigg
Western Isles (Bruce Watt)	20 March 1999	Mallaig–Small Isles
Western Isles	21 October 2000	13:45 and 16:00 Mallaig to Armadale
Alladale Lass (cabin cruiser)	3–5 June 2001	Mallaig–Small Isles
Cormorant (Knoydart Estate)	29 January 2001	Mallaig–Small Isles
Etive Shearwater	16 May 2001	Arisaig–Rum and Canna with bus from Mallaig
Perseverance	12 May 2001	Tiree–Staffa
Western Isles	29 January 2001	Mallaig–Armadale
Western Isles	29 May 2001	Mallaig–Eigg and Muck
Western Isles	27 Sept–6 Oct 2001	Mallaig–Small Isles, when *Lochnevis* was being overhauled
Western Isles	17–20 October 2001	Mallaig–Armadale
Ullin of Staffa	11 September 2001	Fionnphort–Iona
Western Isles	19 Oct to 2 Nov 2002	Mallaig–Rum and Canna
Lochan (Bruce Watt)	25–26 August 2003	Mallaig–Armadale
Ullin of Staffa	14–28 Oct 2007	Mallaig–Small Isles Also 13-22 October 2008 and 12–29 Oct 2009.
Sula Beag (Sea Life Surveys, Tobermory)	11–29 October 2010	Mallaig–Small Isles
Western Isles	15 October 2010	Mallaig–Rum and Canna
Orion (Sea.Fari Adventures, Armadale)	9–25 October 2011	Mallaig–Small Isles Also 8–24 October 2012, 14–30 Sept 2013, 13 Sept–10 Oct 2014
Orion	27 April and 1 Nov. 2013	Mallaig–Armadale
Spanish John I (landing craft)	1–7 November 2011	Mallaig–Small Isles
Western Isles	27 September 2013	Mallaig–Small Isles
Brigadoon (passenger only)	17–18 October 2014	Sconser–Raasay

The Small Isles charters were mainly to supplement small car ferries such as *Raasay* and *Loch Bhrusda*.

Left: Red Boat *Kildonan* tendering *Loch Arkaig* at Eigg, 1977.

Above: The last Red Boat, *Dart Princess* off Eigg.

Above left: The final tender at Eigg before the slipways were built, *Laig Bay*, lying on land while out of service.

Above right: *Lochmor* arriving at Mallaig in 1994.

Right: Unloading island supplies from *Lochmor* to the tender *Ulva* at Eigg.

Above: Lochnevis at Mallaig, 2002.

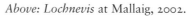

Below: Lochnevis unloading a large articulated truck at Sconser on a special sailing there.

Lochnevis at the new linkspan at Eigg.

Ali Cat in CSP colours passing Greenock in 2005.

Left: *Ali Cat* at Millport on a Clyde River Steamer club charter on 4 September 2004.

Right: *Ali Cat* off Dunoon in Argyll Ferries livery.

Argyll Flyer at the Dunoon linkspan.

Argyll Flyer departs Dunoon, 16 August 2013.

GENERAL NOTES

Liveries

The CalMac livery is a combination of the CSP and MacBrayne liveries, with a red funnel with a black top, and a yellow circle with the lion rampant (which had been applied to the CSP ships since 1965). The funnel colours were applied at the next overhaul after the merger date of 1 January 1973 and *Glen Sannox* did not receive hers until November 1973 and *Cowal* until March 1974. An experimental livery with a yellow band rather than a circle was applied to *Waverley* for a few days in April 1973, but was quickly removed. *Glen Sannox* had a white line at the top of the black portion of her hull whilst serving as the Clyde cruise vessel from 1978 to 1981. The Caledonian MacBrayne name was painted on the hulls between 1984 and 1986. Gaelic names of the ships were added to the forward superstructure in 2002 along with the website address www.calmac.co.uk.

Company Structure

Originally the company was Caledonian MacBrayne Ltd., but on 1 October 2006 a new structure came into being in order to comply with EU regulations. The name David MacBrayne Ltd. was resurrected for the holding company, with CalMac Ferries Limited operating the vessels and routes and Caledonian MacBrayne Assets Ltd. owning the ships and piers. Cowal Ferries Ltd operated the Gourock–Dunoon service and Rathlin Ferries Ltd, operated the Ballycastle–Rathlin service until the contract was lost to Rathlin Island Ferries Ltd. on 1 July 2008. Argyll Ferries replaced Cowal Ferries Ltd. from 1 July 2012. Northlink, serving Orkney and Shetland, was part of the David MacBrayne group until July 2012 when the contract was lost to Serco.

Overhaul Locations

The larger vessels traditionally overhauled on the Clyde, but with the closure of almost all the repair yards there, and the EU insisting on competitive tendering, locations have been varied, with some going to Aberdeen and Leith and others to Cammell Laird at Birkenhead. The Garvel yard at Greenock is still the preferred choice. Smaller vessels traditionally went to Timbacraft at Shandon on the Gareloch and now mainly use Ardmaleish near Rothesay. Some have overhauled at Stornoway in past years and at Corpach Boatbuilders near Fort William.

Left: Queen Mary II dressed overall,
showing her riveted funnel, name
pennant and the CRSC flag.

Right: Finished with engines!
Queen Mary in East India Harbour,
Greenock, 1978.

Above: *Waverley* in the East India Harbour, spring 1973.

Right: *Maid of Cumbrae*, the first vessel to sail with the CalMac colours in March 1973.

Keppel in 1986 showing the metal lion affixed to the former CSP ships. This was the second funnel affixed to her, the first being much narrower.

Above: An unknown Island class in 1995.

Right: Lochmor in 1994, showing the odd colour scheme with the yellow disk and lion aft of the centre, due to her funnel design.

The former CSP sales kiosk at Dunoon, from which millions of stemmer tickets were sold over the years. The building is now used as a coffee shop.

The new CalMac terminal and office building at Oban as it is today, but prior to the construction of No. 2 linkspan.

ACKNOWLEDGEMENTS

The photographs in this volume are almost entirely from the author's own collection. Thanks are offered to the West Highland Steamer Club and Clyde River Steamer Club and for the photographs produced by them. Much of the detailed information has come from the annual review of the Clyde River Steamer Club. The editors of this comprehensive publication over the years deserve credit, as do those who assist in its compilation. They are a great source of reference. Also, the 'Ships of CalMac' website has been used. My thanks go to Iain Quinn for his usual assistance and photos from his collection, and also for proofreading.